II Timothy

TO MY SON

EXPOSITIONAL STUDIES SERIES
by Guy King

II Timothy

To My Son

An Expositional Study

Guy H. King

CLC ❖ Publications

Fort Washington, PA 19034

Published by CLC Publications

U.S.A.
P.O. Box 1449, Fort Washington, PA 19034

GREAT BRITAIN
51 The Dean, Alresford, Hants. SO24 9BJ

AUSTRALIA
P.O. Box 213, Bungalow, Cairns, QLD 4870

NEW ZEALAND
10 MacArthur Street, Feilding

ISBN 0-87508-685-3

Copyright © 1944
Originally published under agreement with
Marshall, Morgan & Scott, Ltd.

First published 1944
First American edition 1971

This printing 2005
This new 2005 edition under special arrangement with
HarperCollins Publishers, London.

The Bible quotations are largely from
The New King James Version
Copyright © 1979, 1980, 1982, by
Thomas Nelson, Inc.
Nashville, Tennessee.

Printed in the United States of America

DEDICATION

to
MY TIMOTHYS,
Norman Cole,
Ted Yorke
Clif Wolters &
John Eyre-Walker

I fear I have not been much of a Paul to you; but, in your different ways, as my young colleagues in the work, you have been splendid Timothys to me.

Accept this book as a token of my grateful remembrance, of my continued prayers, and of my abiding affection.

CONTENTS

FOREWORD

It is not usually considered to be polite to read other people's letters; but for eighteen weeks at our Bible School, we have been venturing to look over Timothy's shoulder as he read this one; and we have made the discovery that, while it all concerned him, almost all of it also applied to us. I have been asked now to pass on to a wider circle what we have seen in the letter, for it transpires that, although it is a private communication, it is nevertheless intended to be public property among believers.

May the Holy Spirit, who inspired Paul's writing, assist our learning and quicken our living.

Guy H. King
Christ Church Vicarage,
Beckenham, Kent.

THE PERSONS CONCERNED

2 Timothy 1:1–2

1. Paul, an apostle of Jesus Christ by the will of God, according to the promise of life which is in Christ Jesus,
2. To Timothy, my beloved son:
   Grace, mercy, and peace from God the Father and Christ Jesus our Lord.

1

THE PERSONS CONCERNED

2 Timothy 1:1–2

THE portion of Scripture upon whose study we now set forth is one of the most moving in the whole of the Bible. Taking its cue from the words of our verse 2, "Timothy, my beloved son," there is a paternal touch about the whole epistle which justifies us, I think, in entitling our study as we have done. It is a farewell letter at that.

I need not remind you that it was written from prison. Paul had a considerable experience of such places—at Philippi, at Caesarea, at Jerusalem, and at Rome. It was the Romans who imprisoned him, it was the Jews who brought about his arrest; but never does he describe himself as a prisoner of Jews or of Romans; always it is "the prisoner of Jesus Christ." It was for his loyalty to the Master that he was incarcerated; and therefore there was no shame about it—but only a glorying in it. One of the longest "stretches" that he ever did was his first imprisonment at Rome, described for us in the two closing verses of the Book of Acts. That was a very lenient experience, as we know. Throughout the whole of the two years his friends were allowed to come and go as they pleased, and he was able to exercise a very considerable ministry. Our point at the moment is that he wrote some of his most remarkable letters in that prison—Ephesians, Philippians, Colossians, Philemon. But all that was, perhaps, six years ago. Much has happened since. He was eventually released, and no doubt proceeded once more on his missionary tours. We have no precise record of his wanderings and doings during that period; but there is every likelihood of his having fulfilled the wishes and intentions that we find scattered about his various letters by visiting the places mentioned. Ephesus, Macedonia, Nicopolis, Crete, Miletus, Troas, Spain—these were probably among the many places where he worked, and some would say that he came even to Britain. That notion is not to be too lightly dismissed, for there are not a few pointers in that direction, as Miss Strode-Jackson shows in her fascinating book *Lives and Legends of Apostles and Evangelists*. At Ephesus, where he had previously labored so long, he would find quite a company of believers; and he seems now to have coordinated the work, and to have left Timothy in charge as Pastor and (though not in our modern development of the office) as Bishop. The same sort of thing appears to have taken place at Crete, where another of the apostle's young men was left in command in the person of Titus. It was to give them guidance for the proper exercise of their responsible duties that Paul wrote the First Epistle to Timothy and the Epistle to Titus, which, with this 2 Timothy, are known as the Pastoral Epistles, or Letters to Pastors.

Then, all of a sudden, Paul was rearrested. Things were not all that they should be in the Roman Empire, and she had come to be nervously on edge—fearful of secret societies and so forth. Among these latter would be the little companies of Christians, meeting in private houses; and we may be quite sure that the Jews did not fail to stir up bitter feeling, and to stoke up the fires of fear, against the Christians. So "the followers of the Nazarene" came to be disliked in many quarters, and it only needed a match to set everything ablaze. That "match," in an almost literal sense, came from the Emperor Nero himself. In his madness, he set fire to his capital city of Rome, and then, in order to screen himself, he blamed the Christians, giving it out that they were guilty of the crime. It is not difficult to imagine the outburst of fury against these already suspected and unpopular people. A great wave of persecution broke forth, in the midst of which that intrepid leader of the Christians, Paul himself, was borne back to prison, to the triumphant glee of his enemies. This time it was to be not the lenient experience of his former Roman detention but the far more stringent experience of the rigor and squalor of the county jail. This is for him the end—and he knows it; yet he is calm enough. He had wanted to "go" before, since that would have been "to depart and be with Christ, which is far better" (Philippians 1:23). His only wish for life was that perhaps he was in some sense "needful" to his brethren. If now that need has been discharged, if now he has finished his course, he is not sad, but glad—his heart is at peace.

Yet, as he thinks things over, he quite naturally dwells upon the little Christian communities that he will be leaving behind. How will they fare? And their leaders—how will they acquit themselves? Young Timothy, for instance, charged with the oversight of the believing companies of Ephesus, with all the extra responsibilities and perplexities arising out of the new persecution, how will he discharge his functions? (*a*) He is only young—round about thirty-six, shall we say; and that is no age for such a task as his. (*b*) He is decidedly delicate—a year earlier, in his first letter (5:23) Paul had counseled him, "Use a little wine for your stomach's sake and your frequent infirmities." Not, you will observe, for sociability's sake, or for your thirst's sake, and, not a lot, but only a little. It reminds me more of the medicine bottle than of the wine bottle! But how will his health stand the strain? (*c*) He is rather timid—yet, like so many such, capable of utmost daring when the crisis comes. Still, the dangers will be very great, and there is the risk of collapse. (*d*) He is evidently dependent— the sort that leans very much on others. Paul is his prop as well as his hero. He is the type that makes a splendid follower but is normally not likely to shine as a leader—yet he has got to lead. He is all right so long as he can turn for advice and help to his spiritual father, but now that Paul is imprisoned and un-get-at-able he will be feeling very lonely and very lost. How well able is our God to overrule all these personal weaknesses and to make Timothy, as we believe He did, "a good soldier of Jesus Christ," ready to "endure hardship" in the Great Campaign (2:3). Well, Paul will send him a letter to cheer and to encourage him—a letter that, so far as we know, turns out to be the last that he ever wrote. "Only Luke is with me," says Paul in 4:11, so presumably it was to Dr. Luke that the letter was dictated. He would have this especial interest in acting as his leader's amanuensis on this occasion, that he too knew Timothy well, and, as the physician of the party when they traveled about together doubtless prescribed for the young man's ailments. Yes—like Paul—Luke would have a soft spot in his heart for Timothy, and would be only too glad to "take down" and to transcribe this great communication for him.

Just at the moment, we are concerned with the opening passages which, as we have said, describe the persons concerned. In the course of the whole epistle no less than twenty-nine people are mentioned by name; and here, in these first two verses, we have the three who are the principal concern of the letter; and first there is—

The Old Man Who Is the Writer

"Paul the aged" is his own description of himself in Philemon 9. That was written six years before this when Paul was only just turned sixty; and unless, as some think, the word should be "the ambassador," we are presented to a man old before his time. He had always lived at a great pace, never sparing himself, always putting everything into everything. It was with him as it was with his Master, of whom the Jews said (John 8:57), "You are not yet fifty years old," when He was only just over thirty!

So he commences to dictate, "Paul"—for, unlike ourselves the Eastern letter-writer always began with his name. (*a*) *The use of his name* serves several purposes. It reminds us, for one thing, that the letter is a human document. When the Holy Spirit, according to 2 Peter 1:21, "moved" the "holy men of God" to write the Holy Scriptures, His method of inspiration was of such a nature that it did not abrogate their distinctive personalities and reduce them to automata. In mysterious fashion the words written were their words as well as His words: His words as well as their words. Thus we find in all the writings the individual characteristics of the writers. In the case of a man like Paul who wrote several Scriptures, there may appear divergencies of use fully accounted for by the differences of circumstance or by the passage of time; yet, for all that, there is generally a sufficient stratum of likeness of characteristic to establish the author's identity. There are many words in this epistle—Dr. Graham Scroggie says there are seventy-seven of them—which do not occur in any other of his letters, and that is one of the reasons why some scholars have held that the Pauline authorship of 2 Timothy is questionable. Yet how many characteristic touches are here. Dr. Plummer is constrained to say of this supposition of forgery, "The person who forged the Second Epistle to Timothy in the name of St. Paul must indeed have been a genius." It is the almost universal testimony that all these three Pastoral Epistles—for surely they must stand or fall together—are genuinely the work of Paul. Even as they are also the work of the Holy Spirit.

Again, what a deeply loved figure will that name conjure up to the mind of Timothy. The word "Paul" itself means "little"— and he seems to have been rather a little man. Oh, but only in the physical sense: in every other way, when or where has there ever been a bigger? "His bodily presence is weak" is his own confession in 2 Corinthians 10:10; and the first-century description of him, in *The Acts of Paul and Thecla*, agrees thereto: "a man of moderate stature . . . bow-legged . . . bald-headed . . . long nose." No, nothing to look at; but someone to look to! What he had meant, *still* meant, to Timothy! To read that opening word of the letter would thrill his spirit, warm his heart, perhaps fill his eyes.

Note what is here said of (*b*) *The nature of his position*—"an apostle of Jesus Christ." There were times—for example, in the Epistle to the Galatians—when he had to fight for his claim to the title. Timothy will not dispute his right to it; yet, as he is going to speak in a tenderly loving manner, Paul thinks it necessary by this hint to remind him that he writes not only with affection but with authority. So might a king talk to his children—as their father, yet as their sovereign. (1) In the apostolate, he did not, I think, take the place of Judas. There are those who teach that Peter acted impulsively and without divine warrant in moving for the election of Matthias. I can see no trace of evidence in the narrative to justify the theory; and I am quite sure that it would never have been advanced except for a splendid loyalty to Paul, lest Matthias should be thought to oust Paul from the place that he seemed so much more fitted to occupy. But how needless is all their fear and fuss. By the time Paul was ready, there was a second vacancy among the Twelve (Acts 12:1–2), and I believe that Paul took James's place. (2) In a sense, others, too, were apostles—for instance, James the Lord's brother (Galatians 1:19), and Barnabas, alongside of Paul (Acts 14:14). (3) There is still another sense in which it may be true even of us—the word "apostle" meaning a "sent one." We must first become believers; then we are to advance to the status of disciples, for I cannot but believe that a disciple is something further on than a mere Christian, in view of the stringent condition of discipleship: "Whoever . . . does not forsake all that he has . . .

cannot be My disciple," as Luke 14:33 [see also verses 26–27] has it. No such condition is attached to becoming a Christian: surely Ephesians 2:8–9 makes that perfectly clear. The disciple is the "learner"; and the Master cannot teach as He would unless, and until, the scholar is prepared to obey completely and follow absolutely. Now are we ready to take the higher place, to become "apostles"—those who are sent on His errands and on His business? Recall how, in Mark 3:14, He ordained the twelve original apostles "that they might be with Him [disciples, to be taught] and that He might send them out [apostles, to be sent]." In our lesser degree may we, too, be of truly apostolic rank—qualifying for the post by the thoroughgoing quality of our discipleship.

It is deeply interesting to observe (*c*) *The explanation of his appointment*—"by the will of God." Paul did not grasp it for himself, did not pull strings to get it, did not even choose it on his own account. He became an apostle not by his choice, his will, but God's. As the risen Lord Jesus explained to Ananias in Acts 9:15, "He is a chosen vessel of Mine." How happy are we if, by His grace, we have reached that place where, in the matter of our life's work and of its great decisions, we are content to leave the choice to Him. To be in the place and at the work of His appointment is, indeed, the secret of richest blessing and deepest rest. Ours is but to trust and obey; all further responsibility is on His shoulder, not ours! When such a relationship is established, we may humbly, yet confidently, look to Him—to guide us, to guard us, to gird us, and, if necessary, to goad us.

There is revealed here also (*d*) *The purpose in his call*—"according to the promise of life which is in Christ Jesus." "On the lines of . . . ," says Moule; "in pursuance of . . . ," says Alford; "in the service of . . . ," says Moffatt. The force of that "according to" seems then to be that his call to the apostolate was given him for the purpose of his publishing that "good news" of the promise of life to the needy sons and daughters of men. Put it this way: (1)

The water—"the promise of life"; (2) the spring—"which is in Christ Jesus," an inexhaustible Fountain; (3) the vessel—destined to come to the spring and to carry the promised water: "a chosen vessel . . . to bear My name," which is very Water of Life to famishing souls. Oh, blessed privilege, matchless joy—which, in our smaller measure, may be ours as well as Paul's. Thus much, then, are we permitted to know about the old man who writes this letter—the letter of a father to his son. And now for—

The Young Man Who Is the Reader

Young, for it is only a year before that he wrote him in his First Epistle (4:12), "Let no one despise your youth." We shall learn a great deal about him in the course of our studies; but, for the moment, in this preliminary glance, we shall add one or two things to what we have already said. (*a*) *A great upbringing*—is an outstanding feature in the attractive picture. His home was at Lystra, his father being a Greek and his mother a Jewess. It looks as if his father had died when Timothy was but a little chap, and his upbringing seems thus fortunately to have been in the hands of his mother and dear old grannie. The mention of the "faith" of these two godly souls, in 1:5, and the "Scriptures" in the home, in 3:15, indicates the religious tone of the nurture that the growing boy enjoyed. Edersheim, in his *Sketches of Jewish Social Life* (p. 115ff.), gives an interesting account of what his education was likely to have been. Then, in the course of time, two preachers came to the town (Acts 14:6–7). Their names were Barnabas and Paul; but because of a great miracle they wrought they were, on the ground of an old legend, renamed by the people Jupiter and Mercury. Personally I feel they would more nearly answer to, shall we say, Sankey and Moody—with Paul in the latter role, "because he was the chief speaker." Timothy was only a boy at the time, but he was greatly attracted by Paul and deeply impressed by the preaching, the stoning, and the raising of the bold missioner. By the time we reach Acts 16:1–3, Timothy has developed into a splendid young Christian, a "disciple," learning and willing to learn, "well spoken of" by the brethren, and when Paul visits the town again and observes the spiritual growth and worth of him, he takes him onto his mission party. The great evangelist always liked to have young men with him, not only as cheery companions but that they might be trained for the work. John Mark had proved a disappointment; now Timothy could take his place; young Titus was another of them.

There existed between Paul and Timothy (*b*) *A great relationship*—we said that, on the apostle's first visit, the youngster was very attracted by him, but evidently there was very much more in it than that: Paul then led the boy to the Savior. So he called him "my beloved son," and in his first epistle to him (1:2), "my true son in the faith"; and in referring to him in Philippians 2:22, he says, "as a son with his father he served with me in the gospel." There was a very beautiful and intimate companionship between this older man and younger man—this father and son.

And note here (*c*) *A great prayer*—Paul desires of God that Timothy may have "grace, mercy, and peace." It is an interesting thing that, in all the greetings of his other letters, his wishes are "grace and peace"; only in 1 and 2 Timothy, and in Titus, is "mercy" added. In an impish mood, Canon Liddon once said that the reason was that they were bishops, and that bishops had such need of mercy! We shall not be so rash, or so impious, as to endorse the Canon's frivolity. But what depths of meaning are in the words as they stand—"grace," for every service; "mercy," for every failure; "peace," for every circumstance. How Timothy would need them all; how *we* need them all—whether in times of persecution, as in his case, or in more ordinary times, as in ours.

These blessings are to come from (*d*) *A great source*—"from God the Father and Christ Jesus our Lord." Grace from that Fountainhead is inexhaustible—ever sufficient for every possible need as it arises. Mercy is there in abundance in the heart of Love for all who fail and fall, that they may get up and go on again. Peace beyond all human explanation is within our reach from Him who, even as He stood consciously on the threshold of Gethsemane, Gabbatha, and Golgotha, could speak of "My peace" (John 14:27). If only, in actual daily practice, we were to reckon upon the Fatherhood and upon the Lordship—not merely knowing the facts, but behaving as if they were facts, for us personally—what peace, what grace, what all we need, would be ours, and in what rich measure!

But now it is time we turned to think more particularly of the third of the persons concerned here—

The God-Man Who Is the Subject

In the whole of the epistle He is named fifteen times, and three times in these two opening verses: "Christ Jesus." The letter is written by Paul, written to Timothy; but it is, one way and another, written *about Him. He* is the Subject. But then, so is He also the Subject of the whole Bible. Recall Acts 8:35. The Ethiopian is reading Isaiah 53, but he is completely in a fog as to its meaning—what is it all about? Philip explained that it was all about Jesus: "beginning at this scripture, [he] preached Jesus to him." It doesn't matter what scripture you turn to, in some sense or other it will be about Him. The Master Himself "beginning at Moses and all the Prophets . . . expounded to them in all the Scriptures the things concerning Himself" (Luke 24:27). (1) In the Old Testament we have in story, in type, in sacrifice, in promise, in prophecy, the Preparation for Him. (2) In the Gospels, we have the Presentation of Him—in Matthew, as King; in Mark, as Servant; in Luke, as Man; in John, as God. (3) In the Acts, we have the Proclamation of Him, His servants going forth to be His "witnesses" in Jerusalem (1–7), in Judea and Samaria (8–12), and to the uttermost part of the earth (13–28). Then (4) in the Epistles we find the Personification of Him, the Christian life being summed up in such phrases as "to me, to live is Christ," and, "it is no longer I who live but Christ lives in me." (5) In the Revelation we come to the Predomination of Him—the Lamb *on* the throne there, the Lord coming *to* the throne here. So, in very truth, is He the Subject of the Book, as He is also that of this part of it.

We know that (*a*) *Paul is always concerned*—with (1) Sound doctrine, he has no use for spineless teaching; (2) Earnest service, he has no room for idle and selfish enjoyment of spiritual blessing; (3) Holy life, he has no patience with a profession which does not issue in consistent living. All these things will have their place in the course of this epistle, as we shall see, for they are never for long out of his mind.

But (*b*) *Paul is chiefly concerned*—with the Person. He knows that things cannot satisfy persons—not even spiritual things, heavenly things; and so, while dealing with the many things of the Christian life, he is continually bringing his young friend back to his association with, and his allegiance to, Christ Jesus. Oh, that our hearts may be enraptured by Him—that our religion and our spiritual experience may be not merely of any *It*, but of *Him*. "That I may know Him . . . ," as this same writer expresses it in Philippians 3:10. Other knowledge, other experience, will follow; but this must come first, and abide first: "that I may know Him." You recall how F.W.H. Myers opens and closes his grand poem on "Saint Paul"—

> *"Christ! I am Christ's! and let the name suffice you,*
> *Ay, for me too He greatly hath sufficed.*

> · · · · ·

> *Yea, thro' life, death, thro' sorrow, and thro' sinning*
> *He shall suffice me, for He hath sufficed:*
> *Christ is the end, for Christ was the beginning,*
> *Christ the beginning, for the end is Christ."*

GRANDMOTHERLY RELIGION

2 Timothy 1:3–7

3. I thank God, whom I serve with a pure conscience, as my fore-fathers did, as without ceasing I remember you in my prayers night and day,

4. greatly desiring to see you, being mindful of your tears, that I may be filled with joy,

5. when I call to remembrance the genuine faith that is in you, which dwelt first in your grandmother Lois and your mother Eunice, and I am persuaded is in you also.

6. Therefore I remind you to stir up the gift which is in you through the laying on of my hands.

7. For God has not given us a spirit of fear, but of power and of love and of a sound mind.

2

GRANDMOTHERLY RELIGION

2 Timothy 1:3–7

THE young Timothy had motherly and grandmotherly influences brought to bear upon his life, and also fatherly influences: these latter not from his natural father, who, I think, had died when his boy was only a little fellow, but from his spiritual father. Observe, in verses 3–4, how tenderly affectionate the relationship is. (1) *His love*—"I thank God": what for? For just the fact of Timothy; for the way in which he had prospered in spiritual things and grown in grace, and for the very great help he had been in the mission work. And also for the fact that even in prison, cut off from him as he was in person, he could still do something for him, and something big. What was it? (2) *His prayer*—If only we could come to a practical realization of the fact that we cannot do anything greater for one another than to pray! Paul is so thankful to God that, in spite of everything, it still remains possible for him to help his young protégé by praying for him "without ceasing." It is good to notice, in passing, that to "pray without ceasing" was the very thing he told his converts to do (1 Thessalonians 5:17). So here is a preacher who practices what he preaches. Would that all we preachers were as consistent; all too many of us, alas, are somewhat like the scribes and Pharisees of Matthew 23:3 in that we "say, and do not do." To do anything, even to pray, "without ceasing"—with the exception of breathing—seems an impossibility, but an old papyrus letter dug up from ancient Eastern sands helps us to get the meaning. I expect you know that these excavations have, through an inspired discovery of the late Professor Deissmann, thrown a flood of light upon the nature and meaning of the New Testament Greek. In one such, the writer complains of an "incessant cough"—meaning, of course, not that the poor man barked without stopping but with constant recurrence. It is the same word as Paul uses and which indicates not that he is continually at it without interruption, but that he is constantly at it whenever he gets the chance. (3) *His longing*—is another thing that we find so moving here. "Greatly desiring to see you"; the last sight he had had of him, the young man was in "tears" at his friend's departure, and Paul, who was aware that he must soon depart this life altogether, would so love to see him just once more—"Be diligent to come to me quickly," he will write presently (4:9). Timothy, too, would so love such a meeting. (4) *His joy*—in his "son" is evident; indeed, he is "filled with joy" at the recollection of his "faith." He recollects the very day when he led this boy to Christ and recalls his advancement in the Spirit as convincing testimony to the reality of his conversion. All this is in the forefront of the apostle's mind; but in the background is (5) *His anxiety*—lest, after all, this humanly timid young man should fail before the onslaughts of persecution, or sink beneath the weight of the burdens of his pastoral duties. So all the wealth of this big fatherly heart surrounds the youthful warrior in the fight; but our present study is to stress a grandmotherly influence. Paul, in effect, goes the length of congratulating Timothy that his faith is the very same as his grandmother's!

I wonder what the moderns will say to that? Doubtless they will impatiently assure us that those old "gospel bells" are cracked long since. Atonement, reconciliation, propitiation, redemption, blood, salvation, and such like—cracked bells! Well, as somebody said some while since, the way to tell whether they are cracked or not is to ring them. In very truth, those who do ring them, instead of merely discussing them, find that the old sweet music is in them still and that there's no appeal like the old peal. Or, taking a different line, our modern friends will say that these ancient bells need recasting. "We want something more up-to-date. If you must keep to these old-world conceptions, at least let us have them in a more present-day dress; drop the outworn, and outmoded, phraseology." That sounds reasonable enough; but the trouble is that in translating these old truths into new language, something of the old truth is so often found to be sacrificed. In trying to say the same thing in different words, you discover that you haven't said the same thing after all. Anyhow, the keen, philosophically-minded, university-trained intellect of Paul was all in favor of what we have called "grandmotherly religion." Some of its features are hinted at in our passage.

There Was a Faithfulness About It

"The genuine faith," says Paul. (*a*) The genuine article—not merely of the head but of the heart; not just an intellectual acceptance, nor a credal assent, but a complete trust of heart and whole being. (*b*) Faith is variously set forth. You will be familiar with that description of it in Hebrews 11:1—"Now faith is the substance of things hoped for, the evidence of things not seen." Or, in Samuel Taylor Coleridge's couplet—

> *"Faith is an affirmation, and an act,*
> *That bids eternal truth be present fact."*

(*c*) The late Bishop Handley Moule says, speaking more particularly, that "for Paul, faith means faith in Christ." Yes, as we said earlier, he always runs beyond and behind *things* to the *person*. (*d*) It is worth noticing that this quality is spoken of here as having "dwelt" in them—as if it was not just a visitor but a resident; not merely a fair-weather friend, departing in foul circumstances. Some of us Christians seem to lose all our faith when the storms of life overtake us—when trouble comes, or pain, or loss, or bereavement, or failure, or anxiety, or distress, faith in Him seems to leave us; we read of those who, in such sad circumstances, have lost their faith. The children at a Sunday-school outing were given, as they went home, an orange, an apple, a bag of candy, and a text card. Mary's text was "Have faith in God" (Mark 11:22). As she got on her bus, a sudden gust of wind blew the card out of her hand. "Oh," she said, "stop the bus, I've lost my faith in God." Enough to stop any bus! But do not let any gust of ill fortune deprive you of your faith in Him. Verily, it is in the storm that faith should stand us in such good stead. Yet we let it go—just when it could be such a help! Do you recall how when, in the boat, the Master had stilled the tempest, He said to the disciples (Luke 8:25), "Where is your faith?" It had gone a-walking when its presence would have proved such a standby. (e) This faith in Him should be both initial and continual—that first act of trust which, by His infinite grace, makes us His and makes Him ours; and then the attitude of trust which, according to His purpose, is to be the secret and principle of our daily Christian life. Not only are we "saved" by faith, as Ephesians 2:8 teaches us, but also "we walk by faith," as we learn from 2 Corinthians 5:7.

Such a faith is one of the fundamental characteristics of this grandmotherly religion which we are contemplating: faith *in* Him and faithfulness *to* Him—a simple trust; a steadfast fidelity. "The genuine faith," which was the common property of this godly family, and which, please God, is shared with all its attendant blessings by every reader. And then—

There Was a Fruitfulness About It

This was no sterile religion. James 2:20 has told us that "faith without works is dead," and in this old-world faith there is a multitude of works to establish the claim that it is very much alive. The Master said, in Matthew 7:20, "by their fruits you will know them," and here we find such an abundance and such an excellence of fruit as to make it clear that this is the real thing.

Let us look at one matter that seems to underlie our present passage, namely (*a*) *The fruit of personal contagiousness*—the faith is passed on from one to another, one "catches" it from another; and that is a true mark and sign of spiritual life. "First in your grandmother Lois"—I wonder how she got it? Was she a fruit of Paul's ministry? We do not know; but I hazard the suggestion that she was already a believer when the apostle first visited her home town of Lystra. Perhaps, indeed, she was one of that first number of "about three thousand" who found Christ on the day of Pentecost. After all, that group consisted of people gathered at Jerusalem for the Feast from far and near, and when it was over they scattered again, returning to their homes, some of them at long distances. How often, for instance, have people discussed how there came to be a church in Rome. Well, but Acts 2:10 tells us that there were "visitors from Rome" on the Pentecostal occasion. What is more likely than that some of those were among the converts? And then they would go back to their own city and "infect" others for Christ. So the little church would begin with the little company, perchance even the solitary individual, who had "caught" the faith that day in Jerusalem. There is a very interesting description given to us, in Acts 21:16 (A.V.), of a Christian named Mnason of Cyprus; it calls him "an old disciple," and the word used does not confine itself simply to his accumulation of years, like, for example, that one we have already noted in Philemon 9 in which the apostle is named "Paul the aged." The Holy Spirit's word about Mnason is one that would not be mistranslated if we rendered it "an original disciple"—another of the Pentecostal fruits, I suggest. Or was he one of the Master's own results during His ministry? I wonder, then, if this old lady Lois belonged to the same class? Certainly among those attending the Feast were "dwellers" in many of the districts neighboring on her own. Of course, the important thing is, not how she came to know the Savior but the fact that she did so come to know Him. Still, it is interesting to see the way people find their way to Him.

"And your mother Eunice"—I think I can see how it happened to her. Old lady Lois returns home a converted woman; and her faith being of a healthy quality, she longs to win others for the Master. But where shall she begin, whom shall she try first? Why, in her own home, of course; her daughter, Eunice. If only she can win her, what a difference it will make to the home. It quite often happens that people who become Christians, and who have an urge to serve, are perplexed as to where they shall start. The New Testament is clear and positive on that point. Why, this very Paul in his First Epistle to Timothy 5:4 says, "first learn to show piety at home"—some find that the hardest place of all; but none will deny that it is the most natural place in which to start. And you will recall the most authoritative statement of all upon the subject, which we find in Mark 5:19. The Master has set Legion free—in body and, as I believe, in soul as well; and now, even as the Lord Jesus is going down to embark in the boat, His new convert conceives the idea of going with Him on His mission, that he might, in his own person, be a witness to the truth of His word. He would at once go as a missionary overseas: let the Lord speak of His power and let him be a confirmation and illustration of the same. It was a fine thought; and I am quite sure that the Savior was pleased, even though He did not accept what he offered. As God said to David, in 1 Kings 8:18, about the building of the temple, "You did well that it was in your heart," although He did not allow him to do it, so I feel certain the Lord Jesus was glad that Legion thought of going abroad as a missionary even though He had other plans for him: "Go home to your friends, and tell them what great things the Lord has done for you." Home first: that is the divine order, "beginning at Jerusalem" (Luke 24:47)—your Jerusalem, your home town, your home, your family circle. So Lois began with Eunice. And the contagion spread.

"In you also"—we know that Paul was the one who was what we call the means of Timothy's conversion; yet we may be quite sure that he was not the sole means. People are almost always drawn to God by a chain—Paul was the last link, mother was another, grannie the "first." I think some people are especially gifted and used to be last links; but all the links make their contribution. The "he who sows and he who reaps" of John 4:36 are two links in the harvest—he who plows was, perhaps, the first link; and when the golden grain is garnered, all the links "may rejoice together." Let us see to it that we are touching people for God, having a share somehow in influencing them Christwards. If we are not used to be "last links," let us make sure that we are not "missing links" in this great enterprise. Let us covet to be soul-winners, at whatever stage our winning contribution shall be made. So did the godly women of Timothy's home prepare him for Paul to give the finishing touch. The apostle found it easy work to gather this fruit—it was ripe for picking when he got there. Ah yes, this grandmotherly religion was very much alive.

If, for further confirmation, we may stray away from our passage into more recent times, we may consider what I may call (*b*) *The fruits of practical activity.* Have there been any real lasting effects and results from this old-fashioned religion? Some people sneer at it: wait a bit—has it done anything worthwhile? If not, let us all sneer, let us continue to sneer; but what are the facts?

Well, think of (1) Its social conscience. Eminent persons exhort the Church these days on its social obligations, but this was a commonplace among early evangelicals. The abolition of the slave trade, the passing of the Factory Acts, bear witness to the practical nature of their faith. (2) Its missionary heart. There has always been a deep concern for the heathen world "without Christ." I do not observe much earnestness on this subject on the part of our sneerers. But the old evangelical religion sent Carey abroad, and Henry Martyn, and a host of others, and established great societies for mission work both at home and abroad. (3) Its earnest spirit. In spite of frequent accusations to the contrary, it has not been gloomy and dull, but it has viewed life's responsibility seriously as something for which an account must be given to God; it has not dealt loosely and flippantly with God's Word, and God's Law, and God's Day, and God's Things; it has ever carried that grand word "duty" in the very forefront of its mind. (4) Its holy living. Many of its representatives may have come far short of its ideals, but it has ever stressed the urgency of holiness and earnestly sought it. The great Convention movement for the deepening of the spiritual life, which has brought such blessing throughout the world, is one of the results of this old faith. What we have termed "grandmotherly religion" cannot be so unworthy after all if it has produced such fruits. And now for another feature—

There Was a Fearlessness About It

(*a*) *No unworthy fear*—was there. "God has not given us a spirit of fear," says Paul. Yet if ever a man had reason and excuse for being afraid, it was young Timothy. Naturally timid as he was in himself; having upon his young shoulders the responsibilities and cares of his Ephesian church; face to face with all the perils and perplexities of a time of persecution—no wonder if he quaked before the situation in which he found himself. How-

ever, Paul writes to brace him up; he assures him that he need
not fear with such a God above him, and before him, and behind
him, and beneath him, and beside him, and within him. "Whenever I am afraid, I will trust in You" says David in Psalm 56:3;
but Paul would prefer the prophet's word for him, "I will trust
and *not be* afraid" (Isaiah 12:2)—an attitude which, as a matter
of fact, the Psalmist did also himself afterwards take up in verses
4 and 11. We will not dare to criticize Timothy for any tendency
to fear, for are we not also much inclined that way? How often
we refrain from some right word or action because we are so
dreadfully afraid of what other people might think, or say, or do!
Do we not hesitate again and again from starting upon some
good course or undertaking because of that stupid fear of failing,
of not being able, after all, to carry it out or to keep it up! Are we
not constantly halted or crippled in Christian endeavor because
we are afraid of looking a fool! Well, this "spirit of fear" has no
right to be there. As we think of the old worthies of past days,
how completely free they were of all such unworthy feeling.

Of course (*b*) *A right fear*—was theirs. Was it Lord Shaftesbury of whom it was said that "He feared man so little, because
he feared God so much"? The fear of God is a thing about which
the Bible has so much to say: indeed, Psalm 111:10 and Proverbs
9:10 combine to impress upon us that "The fear of the Lord is
the beginning of wisdom." Yet this fear has very little place among
the moderns. You have only to mark their flippant familiarity
with God—a thing so different from the saint's blessed intimacy
with the Most High, which is always accompanied by a reverent
awe of Him. The old religion was shot through with this godly
fear. A number of older boys were out together one time when
some piece of mischief was proposed. On one of them refusing
to join in, a companion said, "I suppose you're afraid that, if he
finds out, your father will hurt you?" "No," was the reply, "I am
only afraid I might hurt him." What a noble response; and that

is, in part at least, what the fear of God really implies. The presence of this fear, and the absence of all other fear, make up together that quality of fearlessness which is such a marked feature of grandmotherly religion.

One last element is suggested by our present passage—

There Was a Forcefulness About It

A distinction is drawn in verses 6–7 between the gifts and the gift; and it is when both the gifts and the gift are duly and fully employed that there comes into life that forcefulness that is so characteristic of old-time religion. Think first of (*a*) *The gifts*: qualities which "God has . . . given us" instead of "the spirit of fear." (1) "Power"—both for defensive and offensive purposes; both for the negative side and the positive side of the Christian life. A power so utterly and so gloriously adequate for every demand that will be laid upon us. Verily, "if . . . God so commands you, then you will be able to . . ." (Exodus 18:23). How shall fear abide when such power confronts it? (2) "Love"—this beautifully balances that "power" which might otherwise be a somewhat hard and harsh quality. Qualities are, in this, like pictures— the one needs to be balanced with another. Hence you get "the goodness and severity of God" of which Romans 11:22 speaks. "I will sing of mercy and justice," says David in Psalm 101:1. So love keeps power in proper perspective and proportion. Yet be it remembered that love is itself the greatest power of all. And "perfect love casts out fear," as 1 John 4:18 reminds us. (3) "Sound mind"—that does not give us an accurate conception of what the word means: the R.V. has "discipline," and many other alternative translations have been suggested. The one I like best comes from Professor David Smith, who renders it "self-mastery"—the "self-control" [not "temperance"] of Galatians 5:23, though a different Greek word is used there. How infinitely more effective is a horse when its wild freedom gives place to a proper control.

What a wholly revolutionized thing will that widespread, sluggish water become if it is confined within narrow banks—able now in its swiftly-running energy to do things and to turn things. It is all the difference between waters dissipated or disciplined that is suggested by this quality of self-mastery. Now it would seem that these three things are not characteristics to be struggled for. According to our passage they are qualities which "God has . . . given us." They are His gifts to us believers; they are there—to be reckoned on, to be acted on. What forcefulness they bring to the obedient Christian.

Then there is (*b*) *The Gift*. We have spelled this here with a capital because it is not, like those others we have spoken of, a thing—but a Person. At least, that is my view. (1) Timothy had been specially set apart through the "laying on of . . . hands." In the light of the constant use of this sign, it ill becomes any of us to make light of what seems to have been a God-given ordinance. Paul himself had been thus "separated" for his life's work, as we see in Acts 13:3; and now he has done the same for Timothy. (2) At that time he had received "the gift of God," the Holy Spirit: that is, as I believe, an anointing of the Spirit for the special service before him. It is necessary to look at the word "through" in verse 6, lest we should imagine that it was the laying on of hands that conferred the Gift. The fact is that *diá*, the preposition in the Greek, when followed by the genitive case, as it is here, may legitimately be a preposition of time. We find it so, for example, in Acts 5:19 where "by night" means of course "during the night"; and the "in three days" of Matthew 26:61 is the same preposition and construction. This gives us, I think, the right to conclude that the laying on of hands does not of itself, as it were mechanically and necessarily, do anything—it is not the *means* of conferring the Gift but the *moment* which God chose for doing so. The distinction is not without importance. (3) In what sense is Timothy to "stir up" the Gift? The verb *anazōpuréō* is a significant one: its main root means "fire," and two additions to it mean "up" (*ana*) and "life" (*zo*). So we have the figure of rekindling a flame. The Holy Spirit is, of course, often likened in the Bible to fire—we think of "the Spirit of burning" in Isaiah 4:4 and of the "tongues as of fire" in Acts 2:3. Though He is always *in* the believer, He may have only a little place; but when we are what Paul calls, in Ephesians 5:18, "*filled* with the Spirit," it means that He has, so to speak, *blazed up* to occupy the whole being. It is our recurring surrender of ourselves entirely to the Lord Jesus Christ that brings about that infinitely desirable state of affairs: this is the stirring up, the rekindling. When the Gift is thus in control, and when His gifts are then in use, we find a practical forcefulness of character which is a peculiar property of the old "genuine faith."

Shall we, then, in view of the hints and suggestions in this passage, be prepared to despise, and even to discard, this grandmotherly religion? Shall we not, rather, seek more and more to get back to it—back to its reality, to its sincerity, to its fidelity, to its humility, to its activity, to its virility. What was good enough for Paul, and for Timothy, is good enough for me.

THE PASSING DAYS
TILL THE PERFECT DAY

2 Timothy 1:8–12

8. Therefore do not be ashamed of the testimony of our Lord, nor of me His prisoner, but share with me in the sufferings for the gospel according to the power of God,

9. who has saved us and called us with a holy calling, not according to our works, but according to His own purpose and grace which was given to us in Christ Jesus before time began,

10. but has now been revealed by the appearing of our Savior Jesus Christ, who has abolished death and brought life and immortality to light through the gospel,

11. to which I was appointed a preacher, an apostle, and a teacher of the Gentiles.

12. For this reason I also suffer these things; nevertheless I am not ashamed, for I know whom I have believed and am persuaded that He is able to keep what I have committed to Him until that Day.

3

THE PASSING DAYS
TILL THE PERFECT DAY

2 Timothy 1:8–12

"UNTIL that Day"—how characteristic of the apostle is that phrase. The thought was constantly at the back of his mind. As you read his correspondence, you note how frequently it crops up; sometimes he deals with it specifically, sometimes it just slips out. In this short epistle he has three references to the matter: here at 1:12, at 1:18, and at 4:8. So, for him, the passing days are shaped and colored by the thought of the coming Perfect Day. In view of this latter, he would counsel his young son in the faith to be—

Not Ashamed

"Do not be ashamed," he says in verse 8; and because, as we saw last time, he always practices what he preaches, he says, "I am not ashamed" in verse 12. After all, what is there to be ashamed about in being a Christian—except it be that one is such a poor Christian. In very truth, it is a matchless honor to be a Christian. In one of the Italian wars of many years ago, the recruiting band was marching through the villages gathering young volunteers as it went, who brought their weapon—a gun, a sword—from their houses and fell in at the tail end of the procession. At one place an old woman, stirred by the martial music, went hurriedly back into her house: she had no sword, no gun, but she had a broomstick—and with that at the "shoulder arms," she joined the march. How her fellow villagers laughed! What could the silly old woman do for the war? She hurled at them her spirited reply, "I don't care so long as you know whose side I'm on." I hope that story is true, for the action was fine! Even if we have nothing but a broomstick to contribute to the Cause, let us bring that and see that there is no question of our allegiance, that all may know that we are undoubtedly and unashamedly His. As for Timothy—

(a) *Shall he be ashamed of the Master he served?* "Therefore do not be ashamed of the testimony of our Lord." There is, as here (1) Our testimony of Him. In these days He is "despised and rejected by men," but in "that Day" He shall be crowned. How easy it will be to honor Him then; but how infinitely more worthwhile to honor Him now in the days of His rejection. Have you not some testimony to give concerning Him? Does He mean to you something that you long to share with others? Is He not a Savior so complete, a Master so amazing, a Friend so altogether wonderful? Tell out, not something that you have read in a book, but what you yourself have experienced of Him in your own heart: this, and this, and this, I have found Him to be. On the other hand, there is (2) His testimony concerning us. To give our testimony in these days will lead us on to receive His testimony in that Day: "Therefore whoever confesses Me before men, him I also will confess before My Father who is in heaven. . . . For whoever is ashamed of Me and My words in this adulterous and sinful generation, of him the Son of Man also will be ashamed when He comes in the glory of His Father" (Matthew 10:32; Mark 8:38). Such is His own assurance. We do not forget that we may actually have some testimony from Him even now. You remember old Enoch, of whom Hebrews 11:5 tells us that "before his translation he had this testimony, that he pleased God." It was on this verse that dear Bishop Taylor Smith used so often mysteriously to challenge people: "Have you the testimony?" For oneself, one feels one can only turn the question into a prayer!

> *"Ashamed of Jesus! that dear Friend*
> *On whom my hopes of heaven depend!*
> *No, when I blush, be this my shame,*
> *That I no more revere His Name.*
>
> . . . . .
>
> *And, oh, may this my glory be,*
> *That Christ is not ashamed of me."*

Well then, (*b*) *Shall he be ashamed of the man he loved?* "Nor of me His prisoner." Time was when Timothy held Paul as his hero as well as his father in the faith, when he was proud beyond words to be seen in his company, to be counted among his helpers—has all that to be altered now that his friend has been thrown into prison and is under social disgrace? No, no, a thousand times, no. Apart altogether from the spiritual bond and the mutual affection between them, this Paul who is so dishonored now by men will in that Day be seen to be held in high honor in heaven—shall Timothy, then, be ashamed of one "whom the King delights to honor" (Esther 6:6)? But let us pursue the thought, for a moment, in a different direction. There is, I think, sometimes a subtle temptation to despise some of our fellow believers—those of a lower social scale, those whose mental development has been sadly arrested, those who are not as "out-and-out" for the Lord as we fondly imagine ourselves to be, those who are physically maladjusted. I often think that some of these humbler or afflicted brethren are going to have a high place hereafter, and perhaps we shall feel happier in that Day if we have not been ashamed of them in these days. But to go back to the prisoner—

how great a privilege shall we count it to have been the companions of God's prisoners: a Samuel Rutherford, a John Bunyan, a Martin Niemöller, a Paul. I am quite sure that, whatever else may happen, Timothy will never be ashamed of his great leader, in prison or out of it. Paul, you need have no anxiety on that score!

Then (c) *Shall he be ashamed of the message he bore?* Need he blush to think that he should ever have preached such things? His message is here declared to be a "gospel," a good news, not as the late Prebendary Webster would have said, "good advice"! We have had more than enough of this latter commodity from our pulpits; what people want is good news, *the* good news. But remember this begins with bad news—the pronouncement of our guilty sinnership precedes the announcement of His gracious saviorhood. Note in our passage *How the gospel is described.*

First, it is closely connected with "power." That is why Paul himself was so proud of it, as he explains in Romans 1:16, "I am not ashamed of the gospel of Christ, for it is the power of God to salvation for everyone who believes"—the word he used for "power" is that from which the English word "dynamite" comes: the dynamite of man is for destruction, but the dynamite of God is for salvation. How immensely powerful is this gospel. If sometimes we miss the old power nowadays, that is not because the strength is no longer there in the gospel, but that we have lost the knowledge of how to use it—afraid of handling the dynamite, we have taken to use soft soap instead.

Next, we observe that through this gospel God "has saved us"—grand old word, though so shabbily treated today. It includes three things of course. As to the guilt and penalty of sin, "you have been saved," as in Ephesians 2:5 and here: it is all over and done with—you are once and for all, and forever, released. As to the power and habit of sin, the word speaks, as in 1 Corinthians 1:18, of "us who are being saved": as a matter of everyday practical experience of the power of God. As to the ultimate connection with sin, we shall be saved, in which sense "now our salvation is nearer than when we first believed," as Romans 13:11 tells us: we hasten on towards sin's complete and final expulsion. What a salvation, and what a gospel! Who is going to be ashamed of it? Further, this gospel brings no merely negative blessing; its positive side is that, in it, we are "called with a holy calling"—if, as Christians, we are failing to live a positively holy life, we are gravely disappointing one of the primal reasons of our redemption, namely, that we should be "conformed to the image of His Son," as Romans 8:29 makes plain. How sadly blameworthy are some of us believers in this connection; how little "like Him" we are. In the Perfect Day we shall be perfectly "like Him," says 1 John 3:2; oh, that in the passing days we might be more so!

Lastly, this description of the gospel committed to Timothy—and to Paul, and to us—makes it quite clear that its blessing comes "not according to our works, but according to His own purpose and grace." There is still a multitude of people, even many church people, who think that acceptance with God is secured by their own merit, that entrance to heaven is gained by their own good works. How insistently does the New Testament combat that self-flattering idea! Although salvation is "for good works"—that is, it commits its recipients to a subsequent practical Christianity—yet it is not "of works"—that is, our works cannot win it. His finished work for us must first be accepted "by faith," and then our continual works for Him must follow as the mark of our gratitude and the fruit of our love. Such is the teaching, not of this present poor scribe, but of the inspired writer of Ephesians 2:10. All this comes according to "His own purpose and grace": because of His infinite grace, He conceived the loving purpose of our salvation.

When did God come by that purpose? Let us dare to take just a few steps into that realm of mystery, and note *How the gospel is prepared.* "Before time began," says our verse 9. It was not a sudden whim of the Almighty; it was "prepared before the face [perhaps here=the existence] of all peoples," sang old Simeon in Luke 2:31. Before the sin happened, before the sinner came, before the sinner's world was—the salvation plan was drawn up and ready. The Lamb, who is the Plan, "was foreordained before the foundation of the world," Peter was allowed to reveal to us in 1 Peter 1:20. That word "foundation" means "the architect's plan." He has the conception of his house in his mind; then he sets about drawing his plans. With his thoughts upon what will be the needs of those who will come to inhabit it, he puts in this and that—kitchen, bedrooms, coal cellar, bathroom, study, lounge, and so on. Our word suggests to us the Architect of the universe first conceiving and then planning this world-house for the habitation of men. All the while, His mind will be dwelling upon what will be their need. He sees them in His mind as if they were already here in occupation of the house. "According to the foreknowledge," as 1 Peter 1:2 has it, the Architect knows that the chief need will be for the provision of a way of dealing with sin—so it is put down in the plan. Even before the emergency of sin, there is the emergence of grace. In the course of time the plan was put into effect and, as our passage says, "has now been revealed by the appearing of our Savior Jesus Christ." Hebrews 9:24ff. speaks of three appearances of Him: "He has appeared to put away sin by the sacrifice of Himself"; He has gone back into heaven "now to appear in the presence of God for us"; and "He will appear a second time . . . for salvation." It is, of course, the first of these that the passage we are studying refers to, the time when He was "revealed" in the unfolding of history as the Eternal and Almighty Plan of Salvation.

See here further *How the gospel is exemplified*—that is, how one example is given of the mighty things that the gospel gives us to declare: the way in which God deals with death. That is, in

Romans 6:23, described as "the wages of sin"; so that it would seem that, if He deals completely with sin, it must somehow affect the fact of death. Two things are indicated: again, the one negative and the other positive. First, then, Christ has "abolished death." Hebrews 2:14 says that "through death He might destroy him who had the power of death, that is, the devil." Abolish, destroy—it is the same word in the Greek; and its real meaning is not "to do away with altogether," but "to render harmless," to rob it (death) of its sting, so that 1 Corinthians 15:55 can say, "O Death, where is your sting?" In the Perfect Day death shall, like sin its foul parent, be utterly, finally, done away; but meanwhile, even in these passing days, it is, for the believer, robbed of its sting and need no longer be feared. Also, to speak positively, He "has brought life and immortality to light through the gospel"—Dr. Handley Moule translated the phrase, "brought out into the light": it was once so dim but now so different. It is interesting to reflect that some kind of belief in an afterlife is found in every race of men throughout the world; often it is very crude, but it is there. That explains the curious burial customs among some people—for instance, the burying of furniture, of a wife, of a horse, even of food, to meet their presumed need beyond the tomb. But it is all so dim. When you come to the Old Testament you find many references, yet even there we are still moving in the dusk. Then, the Savior is "revealed": He dies, is buried, and is raised by God; and in that glorious resurrection the blessed fact of blissful immortality is "brought out into the light." Gather up all we have said about it: what a gospel it is that is committed to Timothy and to us! Who will be ashamed of it, or of Him, or of His people?

Two ways run throughout this life, as the Master shows us in Matthew 7:13–14. On the one highway are so few, and they have had to come down so low in humbling themselves, and their lives must be lived in narrow fashions. Do they sometimes have a certain feeling of shame in themselves when they look across upon that other way, with the great crowds that press through the wide-opened gate, and that enjoy such seeming freedom and liberty? The Master Himself did not hide from would-be followers that the company they sought was a "little flock" (Luke 12:32); but He hastened to add that it was the "Father's good pleasure to give you the kingdom." Let them not dwell overmuch upon the situation in the passing days, but view it all in the light of the Perfect Day. Whither goes that crowded road, and whither that sparse way? The one to destruction; the other to life. Oh, where is shame? Let the believer rather lift up his head in proper pride—not in his own merit, not in his own achievement, but in the grace-given, God-given, privilege that has placed him amid the glorious company of God's elect. Paul, in the storm, confesses his allegiance to the "God to whom I belong and whom I serve" (Acts 27:23)—and verily, they are the words of the proudest man on board. Captain Julius is proud, for he belongs to Imperial Rome and serves the great Emperor, yet even he is not so conscious of dignity and privilege as is this prisoner of his—so humble in himself, so proud in God!

We have been far too long on this first aspect of our subject; we must hurry on to observe another direction for life lived "until that Day." We should be—

Not Asleep

You remember how the Lord warns His disciples, in Mark 13:36, "lest, coming suddenly, He find you sleeping." Paul now offers himself and his experience as a guiding illustration to his spiritual son and successor. (*a*) *He had a work to do.* He speaks of "the gospel, to which I was appointed," or, as he puts it in Romans 1:1, he is "separated to the gospel." Having, for himself, accepted the gospel, he was thenceforth, in some sense, committed to the service of the gospel; but he was not peculiar in that— every Christian is, "By Royal Appointment," in the King's service. "To each his work," says Mark 13:34: this for you, that for me; something for each. "That Day" must not catch us unawares, slothful, slumbering. One of our hymnaries has a hymn, "Work, for the night is coming." The very next one is "Work, for the Day is coming." Well, either way, Work! Then the apostle is our example in that (*b*) *He had a zeal for it.* He did not do his work because he supposed he ought to or because he must; quite obviously, he reveled in it and never dreamed of slackening up. He was always at it—"a preacher, an apostle, and a teacher of the Gentiles": preaching is public ministry; teaching is private ministry; apostolizing is peripatetic ministry. What an impression we get of ceaseless and tireless activity. How utterly amazed this zealous warrior would be at those armchair Christians that are all too frequently to be found in our ranks. Don't you think that enthusiasm in Christian service is a quality that is becoming more rare among us? Well, the next thing Paul lets slip about himself is that (*c*) *He had a price to pay.* "For this reason I also suffer these things." When I find myself becoming more than usually religiously comfortable, I turn to the passage (2 Corinthians 11:23– 28) where Paul details some of the things he endured for Christ. Very rarely can I read those verses without being greatly moved and deeply shamed. My friends, it costs something to be the type of Christian worker Paul was. Whether you will be called to suffer physically or not, I cannot tell; but I am sure that you will be challenged to an expenditure of time, money, energy, thought, ambition, self. Paul does not want Timothy to forget that all-out Christian service involves a big price. Indeed, could he ever forget it, if, as is not unlikely, he saw Paul's mangled, tortured, and supposedly dead body on the roadside by the gates of Lystra as is described in Acts 14:19. Ah, but you see (*d*) *He had a goal in view.* Do you remember how he describes it in Romans 8:18, "I consider that the sufferings of this present time are not worthy to be compared with the glory which shall be revealed." There, you see, is his secret. It was the thought of the Perfect Day that enabled him to endure the hardships of the passing days. In the light of "that Day," he was (1) eager to serve, and (2) ready to suffer. His goal brightens even his jail. Keep your eye on that Day, Timothy—and you, my reader; and I, your scribe. Now let us go on to consider one further characteristic that our apostle would emphasize in view of this upward look, this onward look: we must needs take care to be—

Not Adrift

In Timothy's day there would be many temptations to drift and there are many such also in our day—a danger of cutting adrift from the old moorings; a danger lest the tempestuous circumstances of our experience may loosen our hold upon the old realities; a danger of drifting into calmer but illegitimate waters to escape the buffetings of a more adventurous Christian life; a danger of letting go the old anchors that once held us to the faith. Such things have happened to Christians before now; but Paul prefers to remind Timothy of the other side of the matter, and still using his own experience as an example, he says that (*a*) *The believer is kept.* This is one of those things about which he is "persuaded." There are things about which it is legitimate for different persons to have contrary views, and the university-trained scholar in Paul would make him the very last one to deny the right of difference of opinion in all such things. But on some points he was magnificently dogmatic. Things revealed admit of no question. In free and easy days when, in the religious sphere, it is almost a crime against good taste to profess to be quite sure about anything, Paul's forthright dogmatism has a tonic quality—"if we, or an angel from heaven, preach any other gospel to you than what we have preached to you, let him be accursed" (Galatians 1:8), there's iron in that. I suspect our blood needs a course of iron just now. Even the gentle John is equally certain when occasion demands; "we know" is one of the characteristics of his First Epistle, which, incidentally, was written in order "that you may know" (5:13)—it is, to him, not enough to think or to hope; he bids us rest upon God's word, and then and thus to know for sure. Well, after that long preamble, one of the matters about which Paul was quite certain was that God is "able to keep" those whom He has proved Himself "able to save." The storms of life might strain his cordage and tug at his anchor, but the believer need not get adrift, because God can hold him steadfast and sure.

Yes, but only if (*b*) *The believer is committed*—"what I have committed to Him" is the condition and limit of His keeping power. When going to stay at hotels, you have often seen by the reception desk a notice to the effect that "The Management will not be responsible for the safety of any valuables unless they are placed in the custody of the hotel safe." The safe is "able to keep," but only if the valuables are committed unto it. In this latter event, they are kept safe until that day when they are wanted. Oh, restful, steadying thought: that if we commit ourselves to Him, He will keep us gloriously safe "until that Day" when He shall take up as well as "make up His jewels" (Malachi 3:17). About this committing to Him, Dr. Alexander Maclaren says, "The metaphor is a plain enough one. A man has some rich treasure. He is afraid of losing it, he is doubtful of his own power of keeping it. He looks about for some reliable person and trusted hands, and he deposits it there." And who is infallibly trustworthy but the Savior?

Now, the reason for this complete assurance exists only in the fact that (*c*) *The believer is acquainted*—"I know whom I have believed": the rest naturally follows. It cannot always be said that the believer knows *what*, or knows *when*, or knows *where*, or knows *which*, or knows *whether*, or knows *whither*, or knows *why*—but he knows *whom!* That is the essential, and the supreme, knowledge. You will remember another apostle's farewell message to his friends, "Grow in the . . . knowledge of our Lord and Savior Jesus Christ" (2 Peter 3:18). We should all of us progress from our first introduction to Him, through all the intermediate stages, towards that intimacy with Him which He so graciously and so wondrously allows. When Ned Weeks, the cobbler evangelist who did such a remarkable work for God in Northampton, came to die, he was accorded a great funeral. In a public house on the line of route, by way of explaining to the others the reason for the crowds and the kind of man Ned was, one of the men said, "He was wonderful thick with the Almighty." It reminds one of Enoch, who, amid all the difficulties of his family and public life, and in face of all the opposing factors at which Jude 15 hints, "walked with God," until the day when, as a little child explained, "They went so far that God said, 'It's getting rather late, you had better come home with Me.'" To know Him is to want to commit ourselves entirely to Him, and to be thoroughly persuaded that He is quite well able to keep that deposit safe "until that Day."

Yes "that Day" has been at the back of all our thinking in this section. Paul would counsel us to have the thought both in the background and in the foreground. He says as much to his other young helper, Titus, when writing (2:12–13) that "we should live . . . looking." Do you know what it means to live through the passings days with an eye on the Perfect Day? If you went to boarding school perhaps you would understand; for among their denizens you would often discover those who kept somewhere a mysterious piece of paper on which was written just a series of numbers—say, 50, 49, 48, 47, and so on. It was "days till the holidays"; as each night came, a day was scored through—so the happy day of release colored all the varied days of term; they "lived . . . looking." And what of those wounded prisoners of war who recently were told they were to be brought home? Each day since has been one day nearer the day; that has helped them with the difficulties of the passing days; they have "lived . . . looking." It is our wisdom, our joy, our inspiration, our comfort, to look at everything in life as up "until that Day." George Meredith speaks somewhere of what he calls "the rapture of the forward view." He was not thinking of our present theme; but his words may well abide with us as we close this study.

FIDELITY AND FALSITY

2 Timothy 1:13–18

13. Hold fast the pattern of sound words which you have heard from me, in faith and love which are in Christ Jesus.

14. That good thing which was committed to you, keep by the Holy Spirit who dwells in us.

15. This you know, that all those in Asia have turned away from me, among whom are Phygellus and Hermogenes.

16. The Lord grant mercy to the household of Onesiphorus, for he often refreshed me, and was not ashamed of my chain;

17. but when he arrived in Rome, he sought me out very diligently and found me.

18. The Lord grant to him that he may find mercy from the Lord in that Day—and you know very well how many ways he ministered to me at Ephesus.

4

FIDELITY AND FALSITY

2 Timothy 1:13–18

WHEREVER we go in professedly Christian circles, we find the faithful and the faithless. Even the Twelve were not as faithful as they might have been, and one of them was utterly false. So, however exalted the position we have attained, however advanced our progress in Christian knowledge and experience, we need to consider our passage with real humility, lest we are, or should become, involved in its implied strictures. Let us prayerfully study the verses along three lines. But first—

The Expression of the Ideal

The apostle speaks of (*a*) "*The form of sound words*" (A.V.). What does he mean by this (1) "Form"? Some see in it an allusion to some very early rudimentary creed, perhaps a Baptismal Creed; and it may be so. What we know as the Apostles' Creed was, of course, not in existence until a hundred years or so later— A.D. 165. Since that early time this "Form of Belief" has been recited by the Church through the world, and I am bound to say that I am often thrilled, as I recite it, by the reflection that the saints of God in their myriads have "confessed" it in almost the very same "form." Some Christians greatly deplore having a formal creed at all. I cannot understand why; especially as not a few of them quite cheerfully sign a "Basis of Belief" in connection with some body of Christians to which they belong. I quite fail to see what is the difference between a Creed and a Basis. But let that pass; for there seems no certainty that Paul was referring to a creed at all. The Revised Version translates the word "pattern"; and Dr. Handley Moule's rendering is "model." Probably we shall be on safe ground if we hold merely that it was an outline or summary of Christian doctrine. Anyhow they were (2) "Sound words." This idea of sound words, or sound doctrine, is found only in these Pastoral Epistles—and is there six times. The adjective does not mean "orthodox," as we sometimes employ the word, saying that a man is (or, more usually, is not) "sound"! And don't let us belittle the importance of this soundness of orthodoxy, as some are inclined to do—even ridiculing it. Paul would be the very last man to allow us to think lightly of this quality; the prevailing flaccidity of belief would, I suspect, be anathema to him. A body without bones would be a useless, and an unbecoming thing. We don't want to be *only* bones; but we can't do *without* bones. Doctrine is bones; and it is well to see that they are not deformed—that is, that the doctrine is orthodox. "Sound," however, in this place means healthy, health-giving—ministering, as these "words" do, to the spiritual well-being of believers.

Paul now continues: (*b*) "*Which you have heard from me.*" Any wise and loving parent will take care with the instruction of the child; so has this father been at pains to teach and to train his son in the faith. Knowing the essential importance of imparting true doctrine, he has taken every opportunity that presented itself to convey to his young pupil, in "sound words," the truths by which he lives. Is it not true to say that if we have a real grasp and grip of "sound words" we shall be less likely to be beguiled and misled by unsound words? Is not the best protection against the infectious "isms" of our day to be saturated with the disinfectant qualities of the sound Word?

So we are exhorted to (c) "*Hold fast.*" Because we may be so greatly tempted to grow false to the truth, we are urged to continue faithful to it—holding it fast, as it holds us fast. Hebrews 2:1 tells us that "we must give the more earnest heed to the things we have heard, lest we drift away." Fidelity to the truth, as to the Lord, is something that Satan hates; and he will tirelessly attempt to seduce all loyal adherents. He will tell them that it is (1) Old-fashioned—a thing from which we all are inclined to shrink; we just loathe being, or being thought to be, old-fashioned, whether in dress or in opinions. We are all for anything newfangled; and yet, when you come to think of it, are not the best things in life the old-fashioned things? The sun that drove before it this morning's enveloping fog, the very air you breathe, the miracle of mother-love in the world of nature and in the human family —as old-fashioned as can be! And I am not going to loosen my hold on my faith about God and His things because it is old—of course it is; that is just what I should expect. Another ruse of the enemy is to tell us that those who think this way are (2) A minority—and we do so like to be on the popular side. We talked a little about this in an earlier study; and we saw no reason to be either ashamed or afraid of being with the few, provided we are assured of the truth.

But a warning is necessary at this point, that we should "hold fast" the truth, and "hold forth" the truth, (d) "*In faith and love.*" That is to say, that it shall be (1) Not just formal—rigidly correct. When we confess the words, the "I believe . . ." of the Creed, do we really believe? Is it just an intellectual acceptance of the traditional formula; or have we true vital faith in what we declare? Do we, in practical truth, rely on the Fatherhood of the Father, on the Saviorhood of the Savior, and on the Companionhood of the Spirit? Moreover, it shall be (2) Not just cold—frigidly correct.

We are to hold it fast *in love*; the truth evoking all the warm affection of our hearts. And we are to hold it *forth* in love; proclaiming the truth not in a hard and harsh manner but with a real heart concern that the hearer may be wooed and won by the beauty and wonder of the truth itself—yea, of the True One Himself. It is, alas, all too possible to present the message in a self-righteous and forbidding way; and some of us need to be on our guard about this. Ephesians 4:15 reminds us about "speaking the truth in love"—love for the truth, love for the One who *is* the truth, love for the one who *needs* the truth. Let us, by all means, have fidelity to the truth, but let us see that it is radiated by the right spirit.

The above-mentioned faith and love are declared to be resident (*e*) "*in Christ Jesus.*" Namely (1) As seen in Him. His ministry was ever exercised in faith and love; and those who would have Him as their example will take note of the kindly way in which He worked and taught. Even in necessary controversy, His aim was not to win points but to win souls. There are occasions when it is our plain duty to enter upon controversy for the truth; then must we be especially prayerful that the way we do it may be His way—in the loving spirit (2) As gotten from Him. He is ever the inexhaustible reservoir of every spiritual quality that His people may need; and the Holy Spirit will unfailingly minister the supplies to those who trust and obey.

So, as taught by that same Holy Spirit, Paul unfolds for Timothy the expression of the ideal; and he backs up his teaching by an outstanding example of this fidelity that he urges—a fidelity to the Lord which is reflected in fidelity to His servant. He instances Onesiphorus, a man well-known to Timothy. He recalls his love at Ephesus—"You know very well how many ways he ministered to me at Ephesus": the force of the comparative degree in the Greek here would seem to be "you know better than I." Some of Onesiphorus' kindness reached Paul anonymously, perhaps; Paul was unaware of the source of the gifts, but Timothy knew better, he was quite well cognizant of their origin. Paul also recalls his loyalty in Rome—he "was not ashamed of my chain; but when he arrived in Rome, he sought me out very diligently and found me." Onesiphorus was not just a fair-weather friend who at first onset of trouble deserted him, ashamed to know a shackled prisoner marched through the streets like any low felon. Happening shortly after to go to Rome on business, he searched the place for Paul's dungeon until he eventually found him. Here was a fine fidelity which might well be an ideal for Timothy if ever he should be tempted to be false. Dr. Albert MacKinnon, in his truly fascinating book *The Rome of Saint Paul* (p. 207ff.), has a grand picture of this man. He thinks he went specially to Rome to find Paul and, extolling the sheer courage of the journey at such a time of suspicion and persecution, says "He went to Rome at a time when every Christian was trying to get out of it." The slightly peculiar language used here suggests (1) His absence—evidently he is not at the moment with Paul in Rome, for it says "he often refreshed me," past tense; and it seems equally clear that he was not in Ephesus, whither Paul's letter was to travel, for reference is made to "the household of Onesiphorus" (1:16, 4:19) without, in that connection, including the man himself, while in our verse 18 he has a mention all to himself. Many scholars go further and think that all this argues (2) His decease—they may be right; but we venture to consider that the implication of the language is sufficiently satisfied by his absence, for the present, from either of the two places with which this letter is specially concerned—the place of the epistle's departure or destination.

Assuming that Onesiphorus really was dead, *some* think that verse 18, "the Lord grant to him that he may find mercy from the Lord in that Day," gives us warrant for prayers for the dead. Yet surely the form of the sentence gives us, not a prayer, but merely a pious wish. It seems to me a very flimsy foundation on which to build such a practice and doctrine. The precarious nature of the structure is further suspected when we discover that an expositor for whom we have the greatest esteem has seriously offered, as another argument in favor of the practice, what he thinks of as the "prayer" of Psalm 132:1, "Lord, remember David." That the structure needs underpinning is undoubted—but this is special pleading! It is another illustration of how easily convinced we frail mortals are when we want to be convinced. Whatever man may wish, and from whatever tender motives, Holy Scripture gives, in my judgment, no authority for the custom. To use the words of our Church of England Article VI., the practice "is not read therein, nor may be proved thereby." However these things may be, there is, nevertheless, no manner of doubt as to the character of Onesiphorus. There is little wonder that, when the apostle contemplates his deeds of mercy for the Lord's servant, he should break out with the expression of his desire that he, in his turn, "may find mercy from the Lord in that Day" (cf. Matthew 5:7). So does Paul conclude his discussion and illustration of this grand trait of fidelity; but then he turns to the other side of things—

The Exception to the Rule

Note how he says (*a*) "*In Asia.*" This is, of course, not our modern Asia, with its Arabia, Persia, China, Japan, India, and so on. It is probably the Roman Proconsular Asia, though possibly only the strip of that territory—the part which is called Pauline Asia: the area that would include "the seven churches . . . in Asia" which Revelation 1:11 speaks of. In any case, the capital city was Ephesus. In and around that famous town Paul had spent more than three years of ministry. He had met with considerable success and had gathered around him a fine body of converts and had trained a splendid lot of leaders, as Acts 20:17ff. makes plain.

What grand times they had had together, what ties of affection bound them together. Neither he nor they could ever forget the manifestations of God's power in that place, both in the saving of souls and in the building up of His church.

He adds (*b*) "*This you know.*" For Timothy had, for much of the time, been Paul's assistant in the mission work. (I wonder if he took the children's meetings?) He had been the spectator of all that happened and had become familiar with all the people. And since that time of early enthusiasm, Timothy had now, for some while, been left in charge at Ephesus to consolidate the work, and to regulate the life of the church—he had been set apart as the presiding elder, the bishop of the district. When Paul speaks here of "all those in Asia," so intimately is Timothy by now bound up with them that it is as much as to say "all your Asians"!

Well, how have they prospered? Do they give evidence of fidelity or of falsity? To our utter surprise we read (*c*) "*All . . . have turned away from me.*" I think we may assume that Paul's arrest took place in those parts, and that, in his needs, he turned for help and affection and encouragement to those upon whom he could so surely rely. To his dismay they disappointed him, they "turned away." Either they were ashamed of being associated with a shackled prisoner, or they were afraid of what might happen to them next if they were known to be of his company. How deeply wounded he must have been. It is bad enough to be forsaken by any; but those people had been such friends—he had himself led them to trust in the Savior, he had been such an enormous blessing to them—and to think that they should, in the crisis, prove themselves so false! How wonderfully would the Master enter into all that His servant was feeling and suffering. For He, too, had been arrested and "all the disciples forsook Him and fled" (Matthew 26:56). How precious it is to the Christian, in his time of sorrow, and disappointment, and misrepresentation, and suspicion, and loneliness, to know that he has the understanding sympathy of the Lord. It must have meant much, so much, to Paul just then. As Horatius Bonar has it—

> *"Men heed thee, love thee, praise thee not;*
> *The Master praises—what are men?"*

As in the former case, Paul again brings forward a personal illustration and names two outstanding instances of this despicable behavior: Phygelus (one "l," say the pundits) and Hermogenes. They couldn't help their ugly names, of course; but they could have helped their ugly character. Two things only do we know about them: (1) They were believers—or, so I think; and (2) They were deserters—not necessarily from the Lord, but certainly from His servant, and we do not forget that loyalty to *Him* and loyalty to *His* generally go together. Yes, but if, in any sense or in any degree, any one of us is conscious of deserting Him or of being false to Him, let us take it home to us that that need not be the end of the story. John Mark was a deserter; but, thank God, he had the grace of repentance, and he came back—to do such valiant service for his Lord. Simon Peter was a deserter; but, thank God, he too had a mind to return—unlike Judas who "went and hanged himself" in bitter remorse, he "went out and wept bitterly" (Matthew 27:5; 26:75), and that was the sign and measure of his repentance. He came back, to become so courageous and consecrated a follower. Alas, that the two evil examples of our passage did not repent and return, but apparently ended their career in the deserters' camp. What a dreadful reputation to leave behind—a believer, but a deserter! How we shrink from it; how we long to be utterly loyal. But how? The apostle leaves us in no doubt, as, looking over Timothy's shoulder while he reads his letter, we too follow the words that bring to us—

The Exhibition of the Power

Says he (*a*) "*That good thing which was committed to you*" (v. 14). And what was that? Obviously: "The truth as it is in Jesus" (Ephesians 4:21, A.V.); "The light of the gospel of the glory of Christ" (2 Corinthians 4:4); "This treasure in earthen vessels" (2 Corinthians 4:7). What an amazing privilege that all we believers should have all this for the rapturous delight of our hearts, and for the complete satisfaction of our spirit's longings! What an enormous responsibility that we are entrusted with it all for others—we are trustees, we are "stewards of the manifold grace of God" (1 Peter 4:10); and "it is required in stewards that one be found faithful" (1 Corinthians 4:2).

This, then, we are to (*b*) "*Keep.*" But again we ask, How? We are such "earthen vessels," so liable to crack under the impact of the forces against us. (1) Ridicule—how difficult we find it to stand being laughed at; this is one of the evil one's most devastating weapons. More deserters are made from fear of it than from almost any other cause. (2) Opposition—in friendly circles we so happily maintain our keenness, but we so easily crumple up at the least danger of opposition. Faithful in the church; faithless in the office—that is, alas, so often the sad story. (3) Monotony—it is all very well when there is a measure of excitement abroad, a fine, successful mission, perhaps, or a deeply stirring convention; our faces are radiant, our hearts aglow; in Plato's words we "walk on air." But then we come down at last to plain earth again—the glow of Sunday night is followed by the gloom of Monday morning, and all our keenness seems to evaporate. Is that it? "Be . . . fervent in spirit," says Romans 12:11 to the fully surrendered soul of verses 1 and 2, and a beautiful rendering of that is "Maintain the spiritual glow." Yes, "keep" it going, "keep" it up—when life has returned to the ordinary humdrum of the commonplace. (4) Temptation—shows no sign of diminishing; new allurements come to accompany the old; and if we know not where to look for the victory (such as, for instance, in Psalm 25:15) we are overcome and even overwhelmed, and in despair we give the whole thing up.

Yes, it is this keeping that is the problem. Let us, then, assure ourselves that because, as we saw in our last study, He is "able to keep what I have committed to Him," I, on my part, am able to keep "that good thing which was committed to" me. And this is possible to us (c) *"By the Holy Spirit."* It is a most interesting and most heartening thing to notice how the Holy Spirit is meant to be everything to the believer during this age, in order that the Lord Jesus Christ may be glorified—what we ought to say, what we ought to do, what we ought to be: the qualities essential for all this are all found in the Scriptures linked up with the Spirit. In Him is all our possibility for everything. Take just one illustration, as bearing upon the subject before us. In Acts 4 the rulers in Jerusalem have Peter and John before them and command the apostles to cease from preaching Jesus—indeed, they "threaten them," and "further threaten," with dire results if they disobey! The two soon afterward gathered with the company of believers and reported all that happened and all that was said. What shall be done? Shall they be frightened out of their loyalty; shall they, by silence, be disobedient to their Lord, false to His cause? Well, they went to prayer; and this was the burden of their petition: "Now, Lord, look on their threats, and grant to Your servants . . ." —What? Wisdom to keep their mouths shut? No, indeed! ". . . that with all boldness they may speak Your word." Not for one moment did they contemplate falsity. Note, then, how their fidelity was inspired and empowered: it is in verse 31: "They were all filled with the Holy Spirit, and they spoke the word of God with boldness." In Him is our power to avoid falsity and to avow fidelity.

A final word on (d) *"who dwells in us."* He does not say "in you," as the run of the sentence might have led us to expect; but "in us"—bracketing himself and Timothy together lest it should be supposed that the Spirit's indwelling was only for apostles, whereas it is, in reality, for all believers alike, "in us": you, Timothy; me, Paul; and all others. It is even true of the unsatisfactory Christian, if he is a Christian at all. It was to a very low level of Christians that Paul said in 1 Corinthians 6:19, "the Holy Spirit . . . is in you." They ought not to have been unholy, seeing that the Holy One was there; they need not have been unholy, seeing that the Holy One was there, with all His power available to the believer for his holiness. But the fact remained that He was there, even though they were unholy. By our unchristian behavior we may "grieve" Him (Ephesians 4:30); we may "quench" Him (1 Thessalonians 5:19); but we shall not drive Him away—He remains in even such unsatisfactory Christians as those Corinthians. How sobering is the thought; but how strengthening. If He be there, then all is within my reach. Yes; but if we are to tap His mighty resources, He must be not only Resident, but President— He must not only have a place, but the whole place; which is what being "filled with the Spirit" means in Ephesians 5:18. Let us, then, habitually and by faith draw upon Him for the power for unswerving fidelity.

In his exhaustive book on *The Holy Spirit of God*, that great evangelical theologian, the late Dr. W. H. Griffith Thomas, says, "There are three special features of Christianity in relation to the individual. The first is Conversion . . . the second is Communion with God . . . the third is Character. . . . Now it is the peculiar province of the Holy Spirit to provide and make real these three essential needs of man." We will add but this, that having begun in us from the first step, He abides in us that, by our letting Him free to function within us, He may enable us for those other steps in the pathway of utter fidelity.

SOME THINGS
EVERY CHRISTIAN
SHOULD UNDERSTAND

2 Timothy 2:1–7

1. You therefore, my son, be strong in the grace that is in Christ Jesus.
2. And the things that you have heard from me among many witnesses, commit these to faithful men who will be able to teach others also.
3. You therefore must endure hardship as a good soldier of Jesus Christ.
4. No one engaged in warfare entangles himself with the affairs of this life, that he may please him who enlisted him as a soldier.
5. And also if anyone competes in athletics, he is not crowned unless he competes according to the rules.
6. The hard-working farmer must be first to partake of the crops.
7. Consider what I say, and may the Lord give you understanding in all things.

SOME THINGS EVERY CHRISTIAN SHOULD UNDERSTAND

2 Timothy 2:1–7

IN THE closing verse of our passage there are two things of fundamental importance. The first is in that word "consider." One of the troubles nowadays is that, in the rush and hurry of life, we are largely losing the capacity to think because we will not take time to do it. Even we Christians are, because of the pressure of things, curtailing our private meditations; and, by reason of the prevailing fashion of short snippety sermons, we are so starved of spiritual provender that we rarely "consider" even God's things. The word of Job 37:14, "Stand still, and consider . . . ," is essentially a word for today. Then, that other word, "understanding": The ordinary natural man does not, and cannot, grasp God's things, "because they are spiritually discerned" (1 Corinthians 2:14); but we who are spiritual should seek by the Spirit to attain to spiritual discernment—not only to observe His "acts," but to recognize His "ways" (Psalm 103:7)—that is, to understand. Well, verses 2–6 of our present portion contain matters which we believers certainly ought to comprehend: for instance—

The Strategic Nature of the Christian Position

If you are a Christian you are, in your measure and in your circumstances, responsible for propagating the truth and for passing on the life. See here (*a*) *The links in the chain.* The truth is (1) given to Paul; then, through him (2) given to Timothy; then, through him (3) given to "faithful men"; then through them (4) given to "others also." Every soul won is a new center of influence. You see that strikingly working itself out in the case of Andrew and the rest in John 1. Here is another striking instance. Richard Sibbes, an old Puritan, wrote a little book called *The Bruised Reed.* One day it fell into the hands of a tin peddler who gave it to a boy called Richard Baxter, who, through reading it, became in time the saintly Richard Baxter of Kidderminster. In process of time Baxter wrote *A Call to the Unconverted,* and by doing so kindled the flame in the heart of Philip Doddridge, who in turn wrote a book called *The Rise and Progress of Religion in the Soul.* This fell into the hands of William Wilberforce, changed his life, and led the great emancipator of the slaves to write *A Practical View of Christianity.* By reading this the heart of Leigh Richmond underwent a strange blossoming, and, as one result, he wrote *The Dairyman's Daughter,* which besides being the most powerful religious influence in the life of Queen Victoria, had a good deal to do with the transformation of Thomas Chalmers, who in his turn touched the whole world. Precious chain! Every Christian thus occupies a strategic position; in modern phrase, he is a "cell," a new center of influence.

Look for a moment at (*b*) *The time of Timothy's getting it.* "In the presence of [a legitimate rendering of the word here translated "among"] many witnesses" gives us a probable clue. Evidently it was at the time of his ordination, his setting apart "through the laying on of my hands" (1:6); but it was not only Paul's hands, "the laying on of the hands of the presbytery" (1 Timothy 4:14) is also recorded. It looks as if, at that solemn

service, there was included a public reading and a public convey-
ance to Timothy of that summary of Christian doctrine which
Paul has called "the pattern of sound words." It was for the dissemination of this body of truth that Timothy was that day set
apart—"in the presence of many witnesses," those presbyters and
others. And if the young bishop should ever waver, there were
plenty of such witnesses to remind him of the solemn occasion
and of the solemn trust that was there and then committed to
him.

So (c) *The responsibility of passing it on*—was once again pressed
upon him. (1) "*Commit these . . .*"—we have already had the
word in 1:12 and 1:14: we commit the deposit of ourselves to
God; He commits the deposit of truth to us and now we are, as
Timothy, to commit that same deposit to others. (2) "To faithful men"—those whose integrity and fidelity is to be relied upon,
who will not swerve aside from any fear or favor, and who have
this further gift, that they are (3) "Able to teach others"—so is
the church advanced, and instructed, and organized; such is the
machinery for safeguarding the purity of doctrine. But this responsibility rests not only upon the leaders, but also on the rank
and file. When I was very young, a few of us got together and
founded a new society—as if there were not quite enough already—and we called it "The P.I.O. League": we leagued ourselves together to Pass It On. In spite of our many and patent
faults, we did understand that every Christian was expected to
"pass on" the News. It was a funny name, but a fine idea. Thus,
through human agency, was the Way and the Truth and the Life
to be disseminated abroad. You know the old legend of the arch-
angel's talk with the Master after His ascension back to Glory.
Michael, or Gabriel, had heard from His lips the story of what
had happened down here—how He lived, and died, and rose.
"And how are the people of the world to get to know about it?"
came the question; and the reply, "Well, I have a little company

of friends there whom I have asked to publish it." "But what if, for any reason, they let you down and fail to do it?" To which the Master answered, "I have no other plan." Man is God's method: He looks to us to broadcast the news unsullied, to publish the truth unimpaired. As a matter of fact, how have we been getting on with it? A missionary was talking one day with an inquiring heathen. He told him of the wonderful Dying, and the wonderful Rising. "And when did all this happen?" was the question. "Oh, about nineteen hundred years ago." "What," answered the pagan, "and why haven't you come to tell us before?" Yes, why not, when the commission was so urgent, when the plan was so clear, when the responsibility was so heavy? All this places the Christian in a position of real strategic importance; but have we grasped that, have we properly understood it? That lighthouse, set up there to send out the light to approaching ships—what a position of responsibility it holds. That wireless transmitter, made to send out its messages throughout the world, wherever it can find a receiver—for good or for ill—what a big responsibility it bears. When the Master says "You are the light of the world" (Matthew 5:14), and "You also will bear witness" (John 15:27), we see again the strategic nature of our position in the world: but *do* we see it? *Do* we understand it?

Here is another thing—

The Strenuous Nature of the Christian Life

It is perfectly obvious from a study of the New Testament that Christianity was never intended to be an easygoing, sit-at-home, arm-chair religion, but a thoroughly vigorous affair. It has, of course, its quiet, contemplative side. Did not the amazingly energetic Paul advise us to "aspire to lead a quiet life" in 1 Thessalonians 4:11? But this is only for our better equipment for the fray. The "hide thyself" of 1 Kings 17:3 (A.V.) is to prepare the way for the "show thyself" of 18:1 (A.V.). The "stand still" of Exodus 14:13 is the preliminary of the "go forward" of verse 15. The "wait" of Acts 1:4 is with a view to the "witness" of verse 8. Let us treasure our Quiet Time with God, let us guard it against any interruption, let us use it to the very utmost—spending the precious unhurried period reading from His Word, listening for His voice, speaking into His ear; then let us get up, and get out, and get on. For the Christian life is a strenuous business—unless the Scriptures give us a false impression. Look at the figures of it that Paul here gives.

We begin with (*a*) *The Soldier*—"engaged in warfare." A soldier has his times of rest, of sleep, of ease; but the whole purpose of his existence is a vigorous one. The word here is not that of a soldier on parade, or on guard, or on furlough, but on active duty. There is a war on, and the man's whole life is keyed up, galvanized into action. That is our apostle's conception of the Christian life; that is one of the things he wants Timothy to grasp, one of the things that we, too, should grasp. And, if we may borrow words used in a different connection, "There is no discharge in that war" (Ecclesiastes 8:8). We can look for no demobilization; so long as we remain here, we are on active duty, with all the strenuous implications of the picture.

Next comes (*b*) *The Athlete*—"competes in athletics." It does not seem quite certain whether Paul here has the wrestler or the runner in mind; but, in either case, what an energetic figure it is. Look at the man's strained muscles, look at his tense face: he's all out! His whole being is thrown into the business of that encounter—as should ours be, who "do not wrestle against flesh and blood, but against principalities, against powers, against the rulers of the darkness of this age, against spiritual wickedness in the heavenly places" (Ephesians 6:12); who are to "run with endurance the race that is set before us" (Hebrews 12:1). And, by the way, that phrase "with endurance" reminds us that our Christian race is no mere sprint—just a great brief spurt, and then all over!

Some of us could make a big success of it if it were like that; but it is the continuing that is our undoing—to keep on keeping on. Like so many of us, "Daniel purposed"; but, unlike many, "Daniel continued" (Daniel 1:8, 21). The "hundred yards," yes we could manage that—perhaps even in "record time": ten seconds of concentrated, almost savage, vigor. The quarter-mile, or longer— that is a quite different proposition; that demands stickability as well as strenuosity. That is our present race: not a sprint, but a long-distance one.

Then (*c*) *The Farmer*—"hard-working." Some poor innocents imagine that a farmer's life is a nice easygoing existence—with plenty of eggs, and pork, and honey, and fresh air, and everything that's nice. Well, consult a Land Army girl and see what report she would give! The truth is so very different. (1) Constant toil—plowing, conditioning, sowing, tending, reaping; always hard at it. (2) Early hours—the farmer cannot afford to lose the first fresh hours of the day, any more than the Christian can dispense with that early morning time with God. (3) Frequent disappointment—frosts, and pests, and weeds damaging the young growth. (4) Infinite patience—for you can't rear a crop, or reap a harvest, in a week: like the athlete, and the soldier, the farmer has to keep on, and on, and on. (5) Perpetual humdrum— there is little excitement about his job, unless something goes wrong. There is a certain thrill for the serving soldier, and for the all-out runner, but there is no thrill for the busy farmer. Such, then, is something of the condition of his life.

There is no doubt, is there, that in Paul's view the Christian life is a strenuous matter? But have we grasped that? There seems to have been some danger—perhaps on account of his delicate health—of Timothy shrinking from this aspect of things and, like the faithful father that he was, Paul would rouse him to a proper understanding of the facts of the case. The state of the world and the heart of the Master combine to call for more "laborers" (Matthew 9:38). At this "eleventh hour" on the clock of this Day of Grace, the Master has to challenge some of us, "Why have you been standing here idle all day?" (Matthew 20:6). He wants workers—not shirkers. And next,

The Sacrificial Nature of the Christian Experience

It was the Master Himself who said (Luke 9:23), "If anyone desires to come after Me, let him deny himself . . ."—say "No" to his self, turn his back on his self, cross his self out. And as we go through our present passage again, we see how completely the apostle has absorbed his Lord's teaching; for if Paul's implied injunctions are carried out, then Timothy's self must go—and our self, too!

It is clear that (*a*) *There are things to be put up with*—"endure hardship." Remember that for Paul's soldier it is not peacetime; there is a war on. He will have to bear the hardship of rough fare and battle conditions, and perhaps cruel wounds. (1) He need not be surprised at this. Old St. Chrysostom said, "It behooves thee not to complain, if thou endurest hardship; but to complain, if thou dost not endure hardship." If the Christian soldier has an altogether easy time of it, he may begin to wonder whether there is anything wrong—whether he is as active as he should be, or so definite, or so loyal. If we are really "out-and-out," we shall almost certainly have to put up with some form of hardship—perhaps from the lack of sympathy in our own family, perhaps from the ridicule and opposition of our world. We must face the fact that while you can be a soldier without hardship, you can't be a "good" soldier without being quite ready to endure it. (2) He will not be alone in this. Our two words, "endure hardship," are one word in the Greek, and according to the best manuscript authority there is a syllable at the front of the word which indicates fellowship—quite literally it is "endure hardship with," which Handley Moule renders "Take thy share in suffering hardship," and which Moffatt gives as "Join the ranks of those who bear suffering." Paul's immediate thought for Timothy is that the young man, if he suffered, would do so in company with himself; that if Timothy should suffer imprisonment—as, from Hebrews 13:23, we know he did—well, so had Paul! There is a certain mystic quality about this companionship in suffering which takes some of the sting out of hardship. That is something of what was in Peter's mind when he urged sufferers to steadfastness by the thought of their "knowing that the same sufferings are experienced by your brotherhood in the world" (1 Peter 5:9). More wonderful still is Paul's expression of desire "that I may know Him . . . and the fellowship of His sufferings" (Philippians 3:10).

Moreover (*b*) *There are things to be avoided*—"the affairs of this life": that is, of ordinary civilian life. Dr. Alexander Maclaren has written, "In Paul's time there were no standing armies, but men were summoned from their ordinary avocations and sent into the field. When the hasty call came forth, the plow was left in the furrow, and the web in the loom; the bridegroom hurried from his bride, and the mourner from the bier. All home industries were paralyzed while the manhood of the nation were in the field." He must not allow himself to get entangled with civilian interests when all his energies are supposed to be devoted to the war. He must, for the time, forswear anything, and everything, that would prejudice his soldiering. A like sacrifice must be seen in the soldier of the Cross. He may find that he will have to give up certain things, certain interests, certain habits, certain amusements, even certain friends—not because any of these are wrong in themselves, but because they are a snare, an entanglement, to him; they get in the way of his success as a soldier. He will not criticize his fellow Christians if they find no harm in such matters—it is not his business to criticize; though, when asked, he is free to give his opinion and to explain the reason for his own avoidance. Anything that interferes with our being the best that we can be for Him is to be sacrificed—however harmless it may be to others, and however attractive it may be to ourselves; even though it be so darling a possession as a hand, or a foot, or an eye (Matthew 18:8–9). Let it be made clear that there are many things in "this life" that, for the Christian soldier, are plain duty: family things, social affairs, business matters, that must be attended to—and done all the better for the very reason that he is a Christian—but the point lies in that word "entangles": that is where the emphasis rests. When anything, however otherwise legitimate, becomes an entanglement, it must be severely, and sacrificially, dealt with.

Also (c) *There are things to be obeyed*—"competes according to the rules." The Christian cannot do as he likes any more than the athlete can make up his own rules or follow his own dictates. In the case of the Greek Games, which Paul was here thinking of, there were various laws to be observed by any competitor who desired to succeed—rules of the track, rules of the training. The one which I find so fascinating is that which requires that all entrants must show themselves to be true-born Greeks; no others were allowed to strive in the arena—even as the Christian race is open only to those who are new-born Christians. That is the first and fundamental law of our running; and there are other commandments following. We are called upon to put aside our own wishes, to deny our own desires, and to perform only His will—"not as I will, but as You will" (Matthew 26:39), as the Master taught us by the blessed example of His own unique sacrifice.

So, by all these various implications, Paul impresses upon his protégé the sacrificial nature of the life to which he has been called—whether as a private individual Christian or as a public leader of the church. Self is to go, every time and all the time. I often think, and say, that self is the believer's main problem. It has such a way of creeping in and spoiling things: self-conscious-ness, self-pity, self-importance, self-confidence, self-will, self-seek-ing. "Let him deny himself"—again we quote the Master's words. This is a law—perhaps *the* law: the law of success in Christian living. This is one of the things that we believers need most to understand—and, having grasped, need most to practice. "I must decrease," says John the Baptist with becoming modesty; and that for the simple reason that it is of the very warp and woof of his ministry that "He must increase" (John 3:30). Or, to quote our Paul's secret, "No longer I, but Christ" (Galatians 2:20). Is any-one inclined to say that this is hard doctrine which we have been preaching? Well—not "we," it is Paul; and really, not he, but the Holy Spirit who inspired him. However, does it all sound too hard and too harsh, too forbidding, all this about the strenuous and the sacrificial nature of what is required of us? All right; let us end on a different note, which also every Christian should under-stand—

The Satisfying Nature of the Christian Service

In spite of the present cost, it is all so infinitely worthwhile. If, from down here, we look on, or if, from up there, we look back, we shall confess how gloriously desirable the life has turned out to be. "I consider that the sufferings of this present time are not worthy to be compared with the glory which shall be revealed . . . ," says Romans 8:18. "He looked to the reward," says Hebrews 11:26. "Who for the joy that was set before Him endured the cross, despising the shame," says Hebrews 12:2. Well, what has our present passage to say about these abundantly satisfying de-lights?

Take that phrase (*a*) "*Partake of the crops.*" That means, doesn't it, that we shall ourselves receive some enjoyment and enrich-ment from our labors. Though it was done for Him and done for others, yet we ourselves shall have gains for our pains. One is forcibly reminded of that beautiful provision in Deuteronomy 25:4: "You shall not muzzle an ox while it treads out the grain." That is a hard job that the poor beast has got, very tiring and very boring; but why take his muzzle off? So that even while he treads the grain, he may eat of the grain. Working for others, he is a gainer himself. While he feeds others, he himself is fed. A beautiful provision of God for His dumb creatures' welfare and, after a spiritual manner, a beautiful rule of His service. Is our Christian work strenuous and sacrificial? Well, our own soul will be satisfied in it. That is the grateful testimony of every earnest Christian worker right down the years.

Then (*b*) "*Crowned.*" What is this about a crown? Why, this is the reward of the returning Lord for His faithful servants: "Behold, I am coming quickly, and My reward is with Me, to give to every one according to his work" (Revelation 22:12). This is the award which, in Paul's eyes, was worth all the "toil and sweat and tears" of his utmost endeavoring. "Forgetting those things which are behind and reaching forward to those things which are ahead, I press toward the goal for the prize of the upward call of God in Christ Jesus" (Philippians 3:13–14). Dwell for a bit on that "*upward*" call for the prize, the crown. Presiding over the Greek Games would be some important personage, perhaps even the Emperor himself. From his "royal" box perched high at the top of the tiered seats, he would watch the contests. When the program was completed, this person would distribute the awards. A herald, in announcing the name of a winner, would call him to come upward to the box to receive his prize amid the plaudits of the crowd—he had successfully pressed toward the goal, and now he has come to receive a prize at the upward call. So will it be when earth's program is done. The Lord has watched us from His throne, as Alice Janvrin sings:

> *"He who died for us is watching*
> *From the skies."*

When the time of the awards has come, He will give to those who have "run well" to the end (not after the manner of Galatians 5:7) the "call" to come "upward" to receive their "prize," their "crown," at His hands. What then will they think of their strenu-ousness and of their sacrifices? The "fruits" now, and the "crown" then, will vastly outweigh any giving-up there may have been. When a man said to Hudson Taylor, "You must have made many sacrifices," the veteran missionary replied, almost angrily, "Sir, I never made a sacrifice in my life." It was his experience of the generous grace of his Master that he always got more than he gave! But, if we want the gains, we must have the pains; or, as Dr. Alfred Plummer said in summing this matter up, "No cross, no crown!"

But there is one more thing which is, after all, better than anything we have already said: (c) *"He may please Him."* What greater glory can a human being have, what deeper joy can he experience, than to win a smile from his Lord? (1) At the start, God chose them—chose them to be soldiers. Do you say that bars you out, because you are so feeble and insignificant that He would never choose you to be a soldier? Oh, but wait a moment: listen to this, "Not many wise according to the flesh, not many mighty, not many noble, are called [He doesn't say 'not any,' but 'not many']. But God has chosen the foolish things of the world to put to shame the wise, and God has chosen the weak things of the world to put to shame the things which are mighty; and the base things of the world and things which are despised God has chosen, and the things which are not [the mere nonentities], to bring to nothing things that are [powers that be], that no flesh should glory in His presence" (1 Corinthians 1:26–29). He has deliberately chosen just such unlikely people, because when they accomplish anything for God it could not possibly reflect any glory on themselves—all the glory must go to God who enabled them.

After all that, you cannot doubt that our Lord is prepared to enroll you; and if you company with those unentangled enthusiasts of His army you will share their joy and privilege, for (2) At the end, they please God. It is a happy thing if we can please others. There is a type of Christian that seems to regard it as a mark of grace if they continually put people's backs up and are thoroughly unpopular. Surely not! If you can please people, so much the better; but always the first thing, and the chief thing, is to please God. One bitterly cold winter's morning, long before the War, the businessmen, warmly and snugly wrapped up, arrived at their city terminus to be met with the ticket-collectors' chorus, "Your transit pass, please!" So they had to unwrap and unbutton, to search in every pocket for the ticket that, of course, they had forgotten that morning and had left at home. Tempers ran out, and strong words, likewise. As one man came to the barrier he said to the collector, "I'm afraid you're not very popular this morning," to which the official replied with a grin, "Well, I don't care, so long as I'm popular up there"—pointing to the office of the General Manager of the Line. Splendid if he could manage to retain his popularity with the passengers, but the principal thing, the essential thing, was to be well thought of by the Company. Would you deem me irreverent if, pointing my finger heavenwards, I say that the thing that counts is to be "popular up there"?—"that he may please Him who enlisted him as a soldier." To receive His smile—what honor, what ineffable happiness, what all-embracing satisfaction. And we haven't to wait till the end to receive it, for, as Hebrews 11:5 says of Enoch, "before his translation he had this testimony, that he pleased God."

Having come with me thus far, do you wonder that both Timothy and we need strength to carry out what has been laid before us? It will have to be a strength beyond our own. Very affectionately Paul reminds Timothy of that strength before ever he shows him why he will so badly need it. In the opening verse: "My son"—it is "my child," really; so affectionately does this father think of his son in the faith—"be strong [strengthen yourself] in the grace that is in Christ Jesus." You will only adequately strengthen yourself when you learn day by day to draw upon His grace which alone is sufficient to strengthen you for a life so strategic, so strenuous, so sacrificial—and with it all, so satisfying. That will be, as we shall see later on, the very last word that the apostle will write to him: "Grace be with you. Amen."

THE GOSPEL GOLD MINE

2 Timothy 2:8–10

8. Remember that Jesus Christ, of the seed of David, was raised from the dead according to my gospel,

9. for which I suffer trouble as an evildoer, even to the point of chains; but the word of God is not chained.

10. Therefore I endure all things for the sake of the elect, that they also may obtain the salvation which is in Christ Jesus with eternal glory.

6

THE GOSPEL GOLD MINE

2 Timothy 2:8–10

WHAT a gold mine of truth and blessing the passage is: every sentence an ingot, every word a nugget, the whole immensely wealthy with the glittering commodity of the gospel. We discover that—

The Gold Is Actually Stored in Christ

In verse 10 we learn (*a*) *That all is "in Christ Jesus."* It is one of the outstanding emphases of the New Testament that everything that the believer possesses is "in Him"; over and over again does this phrase occur, and also the companion phrase "in Christ." You find this thought very prominent in the Epistle to the Ephesians; indeed, I am going to be so rash, and so bold, as to suggest that the many commentators who say that the key thought of that epistle is the phrase "in the heavenlies" might be asked whether they are quite right. Their phrase is certainly the theme of one early section of the epistle; but is not the sum and substance of the whole to be found in the words "in Him," "in Christ," "in the Lord"? All that we Christians need is in Him; but we are ourselves also in Him—so that in Him "our need and His great fullness meet." Imagine a bitterly cold evening, whereon a poor, hungry, ill-clad, shivering mortal is standing gazing into the dining room window of a great London house. The table is laden with good things in abundance (for this is not wartime) and the man realizes that, with what is there and what is to come, all his appetite and need could be fully supplied—it is all in the house, stored up in there. Fairy stories may legitimately take unexpected turns; so, as the occupants of this house are kindly folk, and as they observe the necessitous man and his eager, hungry looks, a footman is told to go to the door and to invite him to come in. Now see what a change is wrought in his circumstances and condition. All that he needs is in the house; and, wonder of wonders, he also is in the house—his need and its great fullness meet. It is no fairy tale—for we are not following "cunningly devised fables" (2 Peter 1:16), but plain unvarnished truth that a like blessed propinquity exists for all believers, seeing that supplies and suppliants are both alike in Him. But our passage goes further—

From verse 8 we deduce (*b*) *That this all is not only in Him, but is He.* The beautiful truth emerges that He not only *gives* the gold but *is* the gold; not only *provides* the gospel but *is* the gospel. Let the first reader of this letter, and every subsequent reader, "remember" that fact—that he has to do not merely with a thing, however grand; not merely with an experience, however glorious; but with a Person infinitely wonderful and blessedly adequate. Note, then, how He is presented here:

(1) His Person—"of the seed of David." It is His humanity that is stressed at this point, for He can only legitimately die for the sins of man if He Himself is Man; the only admissible "mediator between God and men [is] the Man Christ Jesus," as we learn from 1 Timothy 2:5—at the other side He must, of course, be God; but this side He must be Man, and that is the emphasis here. How truly human He always showed Himself to be: it was no pretense, no make-believe. In the home—growing naturally, as other children, mentally, physically, spiritually, and socially (Luke 2:52). In the workshop—toiling just like every other artisan in the village, as the carpenter (Mark 6:3). In the desert—

facing the full force of the devil's temptation like ourselves (Matthew 4:1; Hebrews 4:15). On the road—feeling, as any man would, the pangs of hunger if he left home before breakfast (Matthew 21:18). At the graveside—so closely entering into the grief of His friends as to weep with them (John 11:35). (By the way, only in the English is this the shortest verse in the Bible. In the Greek it has sixteen letters, but 1 Thessalonians 5:16 has only fourteen letters!) In the boat—completely exhausted, He falls into so heavy a sleep that even the violent storm fails to rouse Him. Yes, His humanity is all so real; and in all the storms and stresses of our human life it is a refreshing, and steadying, and stimulating habit to "remember Jesus Christ," as the R.V. puts the opening phrase of our eighth verse. But you will notice that it is not only His humanity that is underlined here, but His Davidic descent. Dr. E. F. Scott, of New York, in the *Moffatt Commentary*, reminds us that "for primitive Christianity the descent from David was most important as the guarantee that He was the Messiah foretold in prophecy."

(2) His Cross—"the dead," is another thing indicated. It was for that He came to take upon Him our flesh. In the deep necessities of things, He had to die; but God cannot die. So He became man that He might have a body to die with—as Hebrews 10:5 says, "a body You have prepared for Me"; "who Himself bore our sins in His own body on the tree" (1 Peter 2:24). But was that death accepted at the Court of Heaven? The answer is in—

(3) His Resurrection—"was raised." It is most important to remember that the New Testament nowhere teaches that, by the exercise of His own mighty power, He raised Himself. Some of our hymns say that; but the Bible never does. He could have done so, as He specifically states in John 10:18, for He still retained His deity; but He did not do so. Over and over again the phrase comes: "God raised Him." On the very few occasions when it says just that He rose again, it is dealing merely with the fact

that He did, not with the power by which He did. I myself think that this is the reconciling explanation of the exception to the rule, which is found in John 2:19. In connection with the power thereof, it is more exactly true to say, not that He rose, but that He "was raised." A familiar illustration will make it all plain. Suppose a man is imprisoned to serve some sentence. Imagine that by his own strength and resourceful wit he breaks out. The crime remains unexpiated, and the law has dominion over him and can arrest him, when found, and return him to his incarceration. On the other hand, think of him as having completed his term and of the warder, the governor's representative, the king's officer, coming and throwing open the door of his cell and the gate of the prison, and bidding him go free. He has made atonement, he has served his sentence; the law has no further hold on him, has no more dominion over him. Let us, in all reverence, transfer the figure to the case of our Lord Jesus. If He had, by His own power, forced His way out of the tomb, we should not have known that the sentence of death was reckoned by God as having been fully and finally carried out. But the Governor (Psalm 8:1, 9, P.B.V.) sent His officer, the angel, who "rolled back the stone from the door" (Matthew 28:2)—and the Savior came forth in token that the sentence was completely served, the debt fully paid, the law utterly satisfied. The Cross was the payment; the Resurrection was God's receipt. We now know that the demands of the law have no further claim or hold upon Him, nor upon us who believe, because we are "in Him"—"Death no longer has dominion over Him" (Romans 6:9); therefore, "sin shall not have dominion over you" (Romans 6:14). Well—in these ever to be "remembered" facts about the Lord, which make Him indeed to be the gospel, Timothy is to find ground for his own steadfastness and adequate rejoinder to those false teachers whom, according to Dean Alford, he would meet, and who flatly denied both the Incarnation and the Resurrection. So is the gold stored in Christ. Then, next—

The Gold Is Acquired Wealth for Believers

The apostle speaks of "my gospel," as if, in some sense, he had acquired it for his own. At other times his stress on it was that it was "*the* gospel." We all recollect his sublime intolerance of anything else being considered a gospel at all in Galatians 1:6–9. Now it is "my gospel": all the gold of it acquired not by his earnings but by his Lord's legacy, and made his own by the acceptance of personal faith. This is (*a*) *For his own enjoyment.* What enormous blessings come by way of the gospel. See it (1) In the nation—the "good news" is brought to a darkest Africa, or to a pagan Britain, and you mark, in the course of time, the almost startling transformation. I wonder what beloved, intrepid Bishop Hannington would think of his Eastern Equatorial Africa today, or King Caractacus, or Queen Boadicea, of the change in their Britain since the days they knew it, in A.D. 50 and A.D. 60. And (2) In the individual—what countless, measureless blessings attend the personal reception of the gospel. The results that follow the acquisition of material wealth are but a pale illustration of what ensues from the possession of this spiritual gold. Here is a house—dilapidated, dirty, a disgrace to itself and to its road. One day, activities are observed, changes begin to appear: the garden is taking shape and beauty, window panes are mended and cleaned, woodwork is painted, curtains and decorations attract attention. What has happened to the formerly repellent abode? Only this, that a rich tenant has come in to take up his residence. By reason of his mind and money he is able to transform the place. Just as the coming of the gospel, in the person of Christ, into a man's heart and life will (unless something is radically wrong) completely transfigure his whole character and conduct. To acquire such gold ministers to his own enjoyment.

But let us never for a single moment forget that the gold is also meant (*b*) *For distribution to others.* As the apostle uses that word "my" he would have us grasp that it is not only a gospel for him to enjoy but a gospel for him to preach—a gospel of such infinite and eternal worth to those others who need it that he is ready to "suffer . . . even to the point of chains," and to "endure all things" that they may have it. *Our* enrichment is for *their* enjoyment. (1) Look at this in 1 Corinthians 1:5, "you were enriched in everything . . . in all utterance." Why the "utterance" in such a context? I presume that the good news of the riches is to be uttered abroad. (2) Even more clearly do we find it in 2 Corinthians 9:11, "you are enriched in everything for all liberality," His liberality to us prompting our liberality to others, that "through us" they may thank God. I take it that we may all say this "my" of Paul's as token that we have, by personal appropriation, acquired this wealth which is open to all believers who will thus have it. But let us underline it once more that this gold of the gospel is not for ourselves *alone.* And then we take note that—

The Gold Is Always Free for Circulation

We have heard of money kept secretly rolled up in an old stocking or locked up in the vaults: there is no manner of restriction imposed upon the distribution of *this* gold. The people who need it are *so* needy that it would be a tragedy, and a crime, to hoard it up and not to hand it on—"if our gospel is veiled, it is veiled to those who are lost," says 2 Corinthians 4:3. So we rejoice to know that it is free from all restraint. "The word of God is not chained," says our verse 9—this phrase is just another name for "my gospel," which in the strictest sense is not Paul's word but God's word. In 1 Corinthians 2:1, he himself describes it as "the testimony of God." It is true to call it Paul's word with all its human and personal qualities and characteristics, but it is not the whole truth: the ultimate fact is that it was given to Paul by "the revelation of Jesus Christ," as he confesses in Galatians 1:12, and was God's word for sinful men. For the dissemination of that mighty word, the brave apostle was now brought "even to the point of chains"; never again would he be free to broadcast the soul-saving, the life-changing message as he had so loved to do and so "suffered" for doing. He was now "chained"—but even yet "the Word of God is not chained."

It is true to say that (*a*) *Age cannot bind it.* On the one hand it is, in itself, both ancient and modern—immensely old, yet extraordinarily up-to-date; age does not tie it to an armchair, nor condemn it to a somnolent impassivity. It is as vigorous as ever it was. Nearly nineteen hundred years have run their course since Paul dictated these words to his son, but the Word, the gospel, has not lost one iota of its pristine virility. On the other hand, its message is valid for both old and young—those with life behind them and those with life before them find in it alike their way to God, their way with God, their way for God. No wonder that the apostle elsewhere exclaims (Romans 1:16), "I am not ashamed of the gospel of Christ, for it is [still, in spite of its age] the power of God to salvation for everyone [of whatever age] who believes." (*b*) *Language cannot bind it.* We take up our Bible and find the Authorized Version so throbbing with life, so instinct with power, that we almost forget that we are reading only a translation, and a not flawless translation at that. Whether the Word as a whole, or the word of the gospel in particular, it retains the original power of the original tongue. The Hebrew, the Aramaic, the Greek—these were the vehicles of the inspiration, but the something like a thousand languages into which it has been translated possess the same power of conviction, conversion, compulsion and comfort. Read, for example, the Annual Report, for any year, of the British and Foreign Bible Society, and you will see how remarkably true it is that, in the myriad speech of mankind, the Word retains its freshness and freedom of mighty influence— language cannot impede that. (*c*) *Persecution cannot bind it.* The enemy has tried to stamp it out. In our own country he has in the past caused it to become a forbidden book, and ardent souls have had to read it in secret places in peril of their very lives. He has engineered great bonfires for its burning, when thousands of copies were consigned to the flames; but some were hidden, to break forth again in due time. It is like a little seed dropped by chance into the soft earth of some roadway. The local authority has been paving the street, and very soon a great, heavy stone has been laid and hammered down upon our little seed to its utter destruction. But wait: is it destroyed? In course of time, the very paving stone is moved by the life-power that was in the seed. In modern Russia the hard, cold, dead stones of atheism were dumped down upon all religion in the full expectation that the Word would be stifled; but we have lived to see that the plot has failed and that the stones themselves have started to be lifted off. (*d*) *Deficiency cannot bind it*. The great power has evidenced itself even upon those who might scarcely have been expected to understand it. There is no profounder book in circulation, and there are parts of it likely to baffle the keenest minds; yet quite uneducated folks have come to a wonderful grasp of its truths and its secrets. For it is ever true that God's things, as 1 Corinthians 2:14 reminds us, "are spiritually discerned," and that, not by natural intellect but "by faith we understand" (Hebrews 11:3). So it is blessedly apparent that the gospel cannot be chained: the worker may suffer even "to the point of chains," but the Word is "not chained"! Now for another thought—

The Gold Is Amazing Fortune for Sinners

Paul speaks to Timothy about (*a*) "*The sake of the elect*"— those who are the beneficiaries of God's choice. How amazing it is that, of His sovereign will, He should elect to save sinners! He did not stay to select the best of the bad bunch, He did not wait until they had been able to improve themselves a bit, but "when we were still without strength, in due time Christ died for the ungodly; . . . while we were still sinners, Christ died for us; . . . when we were enemies we were reconciled to God through the death of His Son" (Romans 5:6, 8, 10). Feeble, sinners, enemies: what a crescendo of disability—yet He brushed aside all the disqualification, and, by the exercise of His divine royal prerogative, He elected us. Us? Yes; if we are true believers it is a sure token that we are among His elect. Do not forget that, as Ephesians 1:4 has it, we are "chosen *in Him.*" If we have chosen the Lord Jesus as our Savior and Lord we may be quite sure that it happened because, first and foremost, *He* chose *us.* Listen to Him, in John 15:16, "You did not choose Me [merely], but I chose you. . . ." What absolute assurance of salvation this gives us, since it depends, not on our initial merit, nor on our subsequent doings, but on His almighty grace and sovereign will.

These sinners, then, as yet not brought in, are the apostle's deep concern: (*b*) "*That they also may obtain the salvation.*" It is there for them; but they must come and get it. (1) We have the Fact of the Gospel—"Christ Jesus came into the world to save sinners, of whom I am chief" (1 Timothy 1:15). By the way, do you feel that that last phrase is but an emotional exaggeration? Well, I suppose we shall always think that until we get as near to God as Paul did. They who are the holiest are the most conscious of their sinfulness. We who are so far off can scarcely grasp that. His coming to die, coming to save: there lies the gospel for sinners. (2) We get the Proclamation of the Gospel—Paul with others beside, and Timothy among them, and you and I also, seeking to let sinners know the good fortune that awaits them if only they will come and "obtain" it. Have you occasionally read this advertisement in the newspaper: "Will Thomas Smith, last heard of at so-and-so, communicate at once with Messrs. Somebody and Somesuch, of Somewhere, when he will hear of something to his advantage"? I would strongly advise Tom to act without delay, for there is a fortune involved. (*a*) A relative left it. Tom had been the scapegrace of the family; but this particular uncle always had a sneaking affection for him, and, in spite of his unworthy behavior, he had decided to leave all his money to him. (*b*) The lawyer advertised it; or Tom might never have known about it. (*c*) Thomas obtained it by applying as quickly as ever he could. It is somewhat like that with this fortune of gold of the gospel—God has made it and bequeathed it to sinners; His servants are to advertise it, that sinners may learn of their good fortune; and then, sinners are to come, and by the exercise of their own personal faith in the Lord the Savior "obtain the salvation which is in Christ Jesus."

Do you remember Charles Kingsley's *Westward Ho!*? What mighty efforts Amyas Leigh and his company made, what terrible sufferings they endured, what losses they sustained, in searching South America for the mythical Manoa and its glittering gold. Disappointed, disillusioned, you recall Parson John Brimblecombe's lament, "I think the gold of Manoa is like the gold which lies where the rainbow touches the ground—always a field beyond you." The gold of the gospel is not like that. It is not mythical, but real; it is not gotten by effort, suffering and loss, but by the simple appropriation of faith; it is not beyond us but beside us, in the person of our Lord Himself. What good news for the sinner; what amazing fortune. One last thing about it—

The Gold Is Authentic Currency in Heaven

Our passage closes "with eternal glory." It has met the sinner very much on earth; it has altered his whole condition by enrichment with supernal gold; and now, at last, it brings him unchallenged into glory. Unchallenged, for his gold is as an "open sesame" at the gates of heaven: that which is true coinage here is recognized and accepted hereafter. You can't get through the gates without paying; yet you have nothing to pay with—not your own merit, not your own deeds, will suffice. Be thankful that Someone Else has paid for your admission—with His precious blood, with the gospel gold.

I happen to be a member of the Surrey County Cricket Club. One summer morning some years ago, as I was making my way towards the Kennington Oval to see the August Bank Holiday match between Surrey and Notts, I observed a boy looking very hungrily and longingly through the Jack Hobbs gates as if he would give anything to go in, but hadn't the price of admission. I paid his entrance, and took him into the Pavilion with me, where, his eyes aglow all day, he spent those hours in unalloyed "glory." Happy are they who, in the sense of Revelation 22:14, "enter through the gates"; their entrance was procured by gospel gold given them by God, so that they called it "my" (v. 8); and they were then admitted not to a day of glory, like my boy friend, but to "eternal glory."

Some years ago I read, with great profit, a little book by that fine Bible teacher the late Mr. George Goodman—one of the brethren commonly called The Brethren, to so many of whom, as to him, I owe so much. This was an exposition of Romans 1–8—a portion that he had made so peculiarly his own. What concerns me at the moment is the glorious title that he gave his book: he called it *From Guilt, Through Grace, To Glory.* What a perfect description of those marvelous chapters. Such is the journey, financed by heaven's gold; and such the journey's end.

Once more we read through our present appointed passage, and as we rise from its perusal, we are constrained to exclaim, "What a gold mine!" This "word fitly spoken is like apples of gold," as Proverbs 25:11 says; in Tennyson's lines—

> *"Jewels . . .*
> *That on the stretched forefinger of all Time*
> *Sparkle forever."*

SOMETHING TO SING ABOUT

2 Timothy 2:11–13

11. This is a faithful saying:
    For if we died with Him,
        We shall also live with Him.
12. If we endure,
        We shall also reign with Him.
    If we deny Him,
        He also will deny us.
13. If we are faithless,
        He remains faithful;
    He cannot deny Himself.

7

SOMETHING TO SING ABOUT

2 Timothy 2:11–13

BIBLE religion is a singing religion: that is a theme that might profitably occupy us for a very long while. We have time only to take up two instances of the rule. (*a*) *First, the prophet.* In Isaiah 12:2 we read, "Behold, God is my salvation . . . my strength and my song." That is to say, in the Lord Jehovah he found the *essential* thing: "my salvation"—the foundation of all else for here and for hereafter. There are very few things that are relatively essential to our well-being; there is only one thing that is ultimately essential, and that is "salvation." So the prophet repeats at the end of the verse what he said at its beginning: other things are nice, one thing is necessary. In God, he also found the *everyday* thing: "my strength"—"as your days, so shall your strength be," ran the old promise of Deuteronomy 33:25; and the prophet tells us that he had discovered that it is all stored up in Him. Then came, also, the *extra* thing: "my song." No one can say that joy is essential to the Christian life; one can be a believer without it; indeed, many of God's children are quite cheerless. But then, God is not content to do only that which is needful. He always adds something extra—for example, His full purpose and adequate provision is that we shall be not merely conquerors but "more than conquerors" (Romans 8:37), and so on. Consequently, He here reveals Himself in the overweight of "song," in addition to the "salvation" and the "strength." (*b*) *Then, the psalmist.* In Psalm 40:2–3 we have that delightful bit of spiritual autobiography: "He also brought me up out of a horrible pit, out of the miry clay"—there, again, is the essential thing; "and set my feet upon a rock, and established my steps"—the everyday thing; "He has put a new song in my mouth"—the extra thing once more. There's no need for the song; but it is a great help to have it, not only for our own delight but also for the blessing of others. Note here that, most surprisingly, we are told "many will see it . . .": a faulty translation, I suppose; "hear it," is presumably what he said? No, there's no mistake: when we have the song, there is not only vocal effect but visible result—the whole being and behavior are happily irradiated, and many are led to "trust in the Lord." For illustration of a song's effect read again Browning's *Pippa Passes*.

When we come over into the New Testament, we find the same thing is true. (*a*) *In Ephesians 5:19*, we are exhorted to be "speaking to one another in psalms and hymns and spiritual songs, singing and making melody in your heart to the Lord": our hearts in tune with our hymns, our songs being directed to God's ears as well as to man's. Dean Armitage Robinson points out that the early Christians would inevitably have to exclude themselves from the public feasts of the Greek cities because of the idolatrous rites and ribald drunkenness so much in evidence there. The loss of all this color and brightness was more than compensated for in the sacred songs of the Christian's hospitable fellowship: wherever there was a supper, or a gathering, there would be sure to be singing. (*b*) *In Colossians 3:16*, we come upon the joyous atmosphere again, "teaching and admonishing one another in psalms and hymns and spiritual songs, singing with grace in your hearts to the Lord"—the heart and the hymn reacting mutually upon each other, and both offering their praise to the Lord who inspired it. We recall the place of song in the great revival movements—of Wesley's hymns; of Moody's Sankey; of Torrey's Alexander.

Of course, some people simply can't sing—they have no voice, no ear; pitch and tone and rhythm are mysteries quite beyond them. For their encouragement, Psalm 95:1 invites, "Oh come, let us sing into the Lord! Let us shout joyfully to the Rock of our salvation"—even those who can't sing can make a joyful shout. I think we may legitimately apply these words to the less accomplished of our songsters. After all, God did make the crows, as well as the nightingales, and assuredly takes pleasure in the performance of each.

Bible religion is of such a fine quality that it can inspire a song even in the most unlikely and unpromising conditions. Let me justify that statement by calling your attention to two phrases in Psalm 77. Verse 2 (A.V.) has "my *sore* ran in the night"—we are little likely to find much joy in the darkness and distress of such circumstances; but verse 6 has "my *song* in the night." He, truly, will be one of God's nightingales! Or, there is that other occasion with which we shall all be familiar, in Acts 16:25, when "at midnight Paul and Silas . . . were singing hymns unto God." More nightingales! Sore and stiff from their beating and from the stocks, flung into the foul and filthy dungeon of "the inner prison," they yet found something to sing about.

Yes, a singing religion; but what has all this got to do with our present passage? Well—note that opening phrase, "This is a faithful saying." It comes also in 1 Timothy 1:15 and 4:9 and in Titus 3:8. The scholars think they are hymns taken from a collection which was in use among the early Christians—sung, for example, in the little services held in private houses (*e.g.*, "the church that is in his house," Colossians 4:15), at the table of the Holy Supper, on their partings one from another, on the occasion of a baptism, on the last journey to martyrdom. Such is the suggestion of Dr. Moule. Professor David Smith thinks he can guess who was the composer of the hymns and the compiler of the manual. Comparing the language of these four with that of the Acts and of Luke's Gospel, he is persuaded in his own mind by the peculiarities common to both that the author (speaking humanly) is none other than the worthy Doctor himself. Of course, there was another hymnbook also in use for the synagogue worship and for the celebrations of the great Feasts. It wasn't a great fat volume with a lot of hymns that were never used—it had only 150, all in constant demand. You will recall a specific reference to this hymnbook in Matthew 26:30: "And when they had sung a hymn, they went out. . . ." As a matter of fact, we know which was the particular one chosen: it was Hymn No. 118—you would know it as Psalm 118. Doubtless, in addition to these two collections, one of the brethren would occasionally compose a special hymn, as people do now—like, for instance, "A Hymn for Airmen." Dr. Handley Moule, in his *Colossian Studies*, suggests the conjectural classification—"psalms, the songs of the Old Testament saints; and hymns, the inspired praises of the Christian Church; and spiritual odes, compositions developed by gifted individuals."

The particular hymn that forms the portion for our present study may very well have been used as a baptismal hymn; for we cannot but see how closely its thought follows the lines of the baptism passage of Romans 6:3ff. And certainly it seems to be very appropriate for such a time, and full of inspiration for a young convert making public confession of Christ in baptism. We shall observe this in more detail as we proceed. The hymn is constructed in four stanzas, or verses; and I think, if we want a title for it, we might do very well to borrow from Rudyard Kipling and call it "If"—for each verse begins with "If." Let us now examine it and see what there is in it to sing about. The opening verse brings us—

The Joy of an Experiential Fact

The fact of the believer's union with his Lord is here illustrated. We are all familiar with the blessed doctrine of justification by faith; not quite so sure, perhaps, of sanctification by faith (Acts 26:18); here it is identification by faith. This last truth is unfolded in some detail in Romans 6:3ff. and in Ephesians 2:5ff. Just two links in the golden chain are here touched on—not merely as theoretical doctrine (no doctrine is simply that, in Paul's hands) but as experiential fact.

(*a*) *"If we died with Him."* Paul, even as he dictates, is facing certain martyrdom, and he is quite aware of it. Timothy, to whom he writes, will also, in all probability, become a victim. Scores of others will follow in that noble army. Many think that this is the death with Him to which the apostle refers. But this can scarcely be the case, since, in that event, the verb would have to be in the *future* tense (as are, incidentally, all the other verbs in the passage) as if to read, "If we shall become dead. . . ." Whereas, it is the *aorist* tense which is, in this one place in the passage, employed as indicating that the reference is to something that has *already*, in some specific moment, taken place: "If we died. . . ." When did this happen? Potentially, when Jesus died; experientially, when we were identified with Him by faith. Do you remember the old sin offering of Leviticus 4? The sinner brings his offering for sacrifice—and first, as he confesses his sin, he lays his hand on, and leans his weight on, the animal, which is then slain in his stead. In the type-economy of God, this all pointed to the personal relationship of the believer with Him who fulfilled the type when He came to be the Lamb of God. The sinner turns to Him, confessing his sin and resting his whole weight of trust on Him—and God reckons the identification of faith to have taken place. As in the old type, the offerer's sin was taken to have passed to the victim, and the victim's death accounted to the offerer— so, on our act of penitence and faith, our sin is "laid on Him"

(Isaiah 53:6) and His death is reckoned to us (Romans 6:2). God accounts it so; let us "reckon ourselves" likewise. It is in this sense that Horatius Bonar sings:

> *"I lay my sins on Jesus*
> *The spotless Lamb of God"*

and Isaac Watts:

> *"My faith would lay her hand*
> *On that dear head of Thine,*
> *While, like a penitent, I stand,*
> *And there confess my sin."*

Our personal faith has identified us with Him; and because He has fully borne the penalty, so also "in Him" have we! Is that not something to sing about? But, further—

(*b*) "*We shall also live with Him.*" This "death" we speak of is not the end, it is the beginning. In the language of Ephesians 4:22–24, "the old man"—that is, the man of old, the man you used to be—is done with, and "the new man"—the newborn man you are now going to be—is started upon his life. It is verily a resurrection life, linked up with His, knowing as an experiential fact "the power of His resurrection" (Philippians 3:10). We have been saved from sin's eternal penalty by His death, and now we are to be saved from its daily power by His resurrection life-power within us—". . . having been reconciled, we shall be saved *by His life*," as we read in Romans 5:10. Or, as we have it in Galatians 2:20, "I have been crucified with Christ; it is no longer I who live, but Christ lives in me"—there is the old "I," and the new "I," and the small "I." If, now that we are Christians, we try to live the Christian life by ourselves, we find how hard it is, and we have so many falls and failures; but if, reckoning upon our identification with Him, we realize His indwelling presence, and get self out of the way so that He may do the living in us and out through us, the life becomes a very different thing. Now it is life indeed; now it is fullness of life; now it is what my friend Lindsay Glegg would call "life with a capital L"; now it is that grand quality of life which, in John 10:10, the Master characterizes as "more abundant." Again we say, is this not something to sing about? And here is another of our happy possessions—

The Joy of a Magnificent Future

Our religion deals with the past—which, for the believer, is most wonderfully accounted for. It deals also with the present—bringing him all he needs for the problems, perplexities, perils, and possibilities of his everyday life. But let us never forget that it also guarantees to him a golden future. "The path of the just is like the shining sun that shines ever brighter unto the perfect day," says Proverbs 4:18. We often speak of "the good old days," and there is no mistake about it, they were, in so many ways, so very fine; but the new days just on ahead are going to be finer yet. In the poet Browning "are some things hard to understand," as Peter wrote of Paul (2 Peter 3:16); but he never penned a plainer, simpler, truer word than when he said, "The best is yet to be"—for the believer, that is.

Well now, Paul continues: (*a*) *"If we endure"*—as some Christians will be called to do. The father and son—writer and reader of this letter—with the long line of those who have endured much for their loyalty to the Lord and His truth, right down to such as Pastor Niemöller, and his confreres, in concentration camps; those who lie, even for years, on a weary bed of pain, unyielding and uncomplaining; those who, in Shakespeare's words, are the victims of "the slings and arrows of outrageous fortune." Many a believer, one way and another, is called upon to suffer. I wonder if they have been able to enter into the brave utterance of Paul, one of the greatest sufferers that the gospel has ever known, as 2

Corinthians 11:23 ff. avouches, when he said in Romans 8:18, "I consider that the sufferings of this present time are not worthy to be compared with the glory which shall be revealed. . . ." What is this far-outweighing "glory"?

In the words of our present passage, it is (*b*) "*We shall also reign with Him.*" An unimaginably wonderful prospect awaits the faithful believer, and among the golden experiences that lie before him is this reigning. All who are truly loyal to Him here, whether that loyalty incurs suffering or not, will reign with Him hereafter. Note three things about it: (1) The Nature of it— "To him who overcomes will I grant to sit with Me on My throne" (Revelation 3:21). It is told that little Prince John, youngest child of King George V, who died at a tender age, used to love to play a game with his royal father. They would go to the Throne Room at Buckingham Palace, and when the King had taken his seat on the throne, he would bend forward and lift up his little son and sit him beside him on the throne, to the infinite delight and pride of the little prince. A very pretty little story, if it is true. But it is something so very much more than just a pretty story that is revealed to believers in this verse. It is actually the case that, in some real sense, the faithful will share His throne and be associated with His reign. (2) The Place of it—"We shall reign on the earth" (Revelation 5:10). I know some would translate that "on" as "over"; but I would point out that we have exactly the same word and construction in Matthew 6:10 (Gk.) as here: "Your will be done on earth." This reigning idea is not to be spiritualized or relegated to the blissful experiences and occupations of heaven. It is to take place in this very world where we now live. Some strange personal revolutions will be seen in that day when, in the words of Matthew 19:30, "Many who are first will be last, and the last first"—when prominent people will have to take a back seat, and erstwhile humble folks will constitute, in a literal sense, the ruling class. Yes, down here. Isn't there an earth sound about the 28th verse of the same chapter, "You will also sit on twelve thrones, judging the twelve tribes of Israel"? And this, from Luke 19:17–19: ". . . have authority over ten cities . . . five cities"? (3) The Time of it—"They lived and reigned with Christ for a thousand years" (Revelation 20:4). This is His glorious millennial reign on the earth. And to think that faithful souls shall have ruling responsibilities during that time! Does that give you something to sing about?

By the way, we can be reigning Christians even now. Do you recall that word in Romans 5:17 which speaks of some who "will reign in life"? For the vast majority of Christians (let alone the worldlings), life reigns over them—their circumstances, their fears, their nerves, their feelings, and so on, are on top of them. But just the few Christians reign over life—they are on top of all those things we mentioned. Having formed the daily habit of receiving "abundance of grace," following upon the personal appropriation of "the gift of righteousness," they have the secret of royal living—even now, while they await their magnificent future.

Next in our hymn comes—

The Joy of a Proved Fidelity

This verse sounds a solemn note; yet even here, if we are on the right side of the matter, the happy note persists. (*a*) "*If we deny Him.*" But can we Christians do such a thing? Ah, "let him who thinks he stands take heed lest he fall" (1 Corinthians 10:12). The Christian life has not removed us from the possibility of temptation: we may grievously succumb. When 1 John 2:1 says "If anyone sins . . . ," it implies that a believer need not; but it also implies that he may. We must be carefully and prayerfully on our guard lest, through needless fear, or through false shame, or through hope of gain, we even go so far as to deny our Savior. Do you indignantly repudiate the suggestion? Well, hear another, and a familiar voice: "'Even if I have to die with You, I will not deny You!' And so said all the disciples" (Matthew 26:35). In spite of earnest asseverations of loyalty, let young man Timothy beware, for he will be sorely tried; let every reader beware, for the disciples' failure might so easily become ours.

May God forbid; for (*b*) "*He also will deny us.*" How awful if He should ever say to us, "I never knew you," as He did to some people—spurious Christians, in their case—in Matthew 7:23. Yes, but this need not be. I take refuge in that "if" of our verse. It is said of Judas, in Matthew 26:16, that "he sought opportunity to betray Him." We have not to seek such: chances for disloyalty abound on every hand—in the home, in the office, in the work-shop, even in the church; but how happy if those chances are ignored, if, by His grace, we prove our fidelity! For remember that every "opportunity to betray" is also an opportunity to be true.

Lack of space must send us hurrying on to consider—

The Joy of an Unswerving Friendship

Before it passes to its glad finish, the opening of this last verse of our hymn retains still the solemn tone: (*a*) "*If we are faithless.*" However, I much prefer the A.V. wording: "*If we believe not.*" The Greek word is, in the negative form, exactly the same as that translated later by "faithful"; and that has induced many transla-tors to render it as "faithless." Yet there is a good deal of weighty scholarship in favor of keeping the A.V. rendering. Ellicott urges it; and, although he so often is at variance with him, Alford, in this instance, pronounces himself as completely convinced by Ellicott's note here. I am bound to confess that the combination of these two expositional experts is quite overwhelming to this present humble craftsman. But we have also to add the support of Sanday and Headlam, whose note on Romans 3:3, I see, takes the same view. Moreover, the same Greek word is translated "be-

lieved not" in Acts 28:24 and in Luke 24:11. And, after all, how
many unbelieving believers there are: they have believed on Him
to the saving of their soul, but there their believing has stopped.
Come: do *we* really believe Him? Let us test ourselves by any of
His words taken just at random: "It is more blessed to give than
to receive" (Acts 20:35)—do we really believe that? "I give them
eternal life, and they shall never perish; neither shall anyone snatch
them out of My hand" (John 10:28–29)—what peaceful assurance of salvation we enjoy if we really believe that. "Lo, I am
with you always, even to the end of the age" (Matthew 28:20)—
do we, like David Livingstone, take that to be "the word of a
gentleman"? "Seek first the kingdom of God and His righteousness, and all these things shall be added to you" (Matthew 6:33)—
pause a moment: do you really believe that? If we fret and worry
about these necessary things of life, quite obviously we just do
not believe what He says. Oh but, you say, perhaps, it is so difficult to believe! That reminds me of a man who once went to
consult Dr. Torrey about a spiritual difficulty. "You know, Doctor," he said, "I can't believe"—expecting him to reply, "And
what can't you believe?" Instead, to the accompaniment of those
piercing eyes came quick, and revealing as lightning, the response,
"*Whom* can't you believe?" Really and truly, it is not the saying
but the Speaker that we don't believe. Tell me now: is it so very
difficult to believe Him? "Lord, I believe; help my unbelief!"

Well, sense the sheer joy of it, whatever may be our own spiritual condition, (*b*) "*He remains faithful*"—an unswerving Friend.
He will always remain (1) True to His word: "He who promised
is faithful" (Hebrews 10:23); "He . . . will not call back His words"
(Isaiah 31:2)—even the word of warning, as in our verse 12. (2)
True to His people, who are exhorted to "commit their souls to
Him in doing good, as to a faithful Creator" (1 Peter 4:19)—one
who will not let down His creatures. (3) True to Himself: "He
cannot deny Himself," our verse 13. Every divine and human

quality in Him is held in perfect poise and balance; no part of His being contradicts or contravenes another part; what He ever was, He always is—"Jesus Christ is the same yesterday, today, and forever," as Hebrews 13:8 teaches us. Here is One on whom we may always depend, however undependable we ourselves may be. If, from sheer physical weakness, or from the extreme pressure of untoward circumstance, or from the insidious oncoming of doubt, or from any other cause, you find faith faltering or failing, turn away from yourself and cling to this, that He isn't faltering, or even altering: "He remains faithful." Even though we are so faithless as to disbelieve Him! What a Friend! What a joy!

At the beginning of this lecture I referred you to Isaiah 12; let me take you back to it, as we close. Note these three words: "say," in verse 4; "sing," in verse 5; "shout," in verse 6. In view of all that we have been finding in today's portion, am I justified in claiming that the Christian has something to *speak* about, something to *sing* about, even something to *shout* about?

THREE WORDS

2 Timothy 2:14–19

14. Remind them of these things, charging them before the Lord not to strive about words to no profit, to the ruin of the hearers.
15. Be diligent to present yourself approved to God, a worker who does not need to be ashamed, rightly dividing the word of truth.
16. But shun profane and vain babblings, for they will increase to more ungodliness.
17. And their message will spread like cancer. Hymenaeus and Philetus are of this sort,
18. who have strayed concerning the truth, saying that the resurrection is already past; and they overthrow the faith of some.
19. Nevertheless the solid foundation of God stands, having this seal: "The Lord knows those who are His," and, "Let everyone who names the name of Christ depart from iniquity."

8

THREE WORDS

2 Timothy 2:14–19

THERE is much said in Scripture about speech, and great stress is laid upon its very great importance—for good or ill. Take this one statement of the Master's as found in Matthew 12:36–37: "Every idle word men may speak, they will give account of it in the day of judgment. For by your words you will be justified, and by your words you will be condemned." This does not mean that we shall be condemned for making a joke, or indulging in jolly banter, or in clean happy fun—perhaps some of us need a little more of the humorous outlet than we at present allow ourselves; but it does mean that our words are to be examined, like our "thoughts" in Psalm 139:23–24 (A.V.), to "see if there is any wicked way" in them, in us. Note the exceeding importance, then, of words. Let us, in that spirit, look at the Three Words of our present passage; and first—

The Perilous Word

You see it there in verse 14, "words to no profit"—they are, as we shall see, not only profitless but perilous. (*a*) *A certain instruction is to be given.* "Remind them of these things, charging them. . . ." Who are these whom Timothy is to instruct? (1) Are they the believers as a whole? Certainly they need instruction upon this matter, and that matter, and all matters, and they who know most know how little they do know. A boy of fourteen, in explaining to me why he was leaving school, said, "They can't teach me any more" with the self-satisfied air of one who knew it all! I have heard of Christians who have, in their own estimation, reached that exalted pinnacle of sublime perfection: you can't teach *them* anything. Well, well. But I think you would likely agree with me that we need constant instruction. Or (2) Are they the teachers in particular that Timothy is to instruct? These would be the local leaders who were placed under the young bishop's jurisdiction and administration. Certainly they, too, would need it, for they who would feed others must heed themselves, as Paul says to this same Timothy in his First Epistle (4:16), "Take heed to yourself and to the doctrine."

We note next that (*b*) A *right atmosphere is to be created*—"before the Lord": that is, as in His sight, as in His presence. (1) Speaking as in His sight. What a difference that makes—there will be a loving care for our hearers, a straight faithfulness with them. Dr. Plummer says, "One is inclined to think that if ministers always remembered that they were speaking in the sight of God, they would sometimes find other things to say, and other ways of saying them." You may on an occasion have been speaking about some man, his words and views and actions, talking in a somewhat free and unrestrained fashion, when all of a sudden the man himself entered the room. That completely changed the whole atmosphere; he now could hear all you said—you were more careful to measure and moderate your words. Oh, that we preachers, when speaking of Him and of His things, would recollect that He has come into the room, the church, indeed that He was there first (cf. "I *am* there . . . ," Matthew 18:20), and that we were speaking "before the Lord." (2) Listening as in His sight. What a difference this makes in the manner of our reception of the message. Personal preferences will not operate so forcefully, and we shall find His word coming from even the preacher whom we dislike or despise. We shall listen the more attentively, with something of the purpose of the old prophet, "I will . . . see what He will say to me, and what I will answer" (Habakkuk 2:1). We shall be alert to catch, through the human voice, the tones of the divine voice. Yes, if instruction is to be given, it is well, to begin with, to get the atmosphere right—that God may grant utterance to the speaker and understanding to the hearer.

Now we are ready to see that (*c*) *An important matter is to be dealt with.* "Words." (1) They can be of enormous importance, as we have already indicated. Often they are of nothing less than eternal significance. Take Luke 1:47: "My spirit has rejoiced in God my Savior"—who can estimate the importance of that little word "my"? Take Galatians 3:16: "He does not say, 'And to seeds,' as of many, but as of one, 'And to your Seed,' who is Christ"—everything hangs upon the one word; indeed, the one letter. Take Matthew 22:43–44: "How then does David in the Spirit call Him 'Lord,' saying, 'The Lord said to my *Lord*'?"—the whole argument turns on, the validity of the argument depends on, that one word. Or let me take you to your early Church history. Some of you will remember the Battle of the Word at Nicaea in A.D. 325; how that, against the word of Arius for the nature of the Second Person of the Godhead, the word which means "of *like* substance," Athanasius brilliantly argued for the word that indicates "of *one* substance." Fortunately, that great young scholar saw the vital issue that was at stake; the heretical Arius was defeated, and the word is in our Nicene Creed to this day—"being of One Substance with the Father." All that fuss over a word—in fact, one tiny letter, the Greek "iota" our "i," which is the only difference between the two words. Yet how much was involved.

However, the contrary may also be said of words: (2) They can be of trifling worth—"to no profit." Alas, so much time, and heat, and energy, and temper have been wasted on "word-fighting" when the controversy has been unneedful and not called for. People have fought and fought over a word expressive of little else than their own personal opinion or preference. It is a little difficult to decide whether the apostle is thinking here merely of a word or of an argument. I was interested to read that Moffatt's translation of these words runs: "Adjure them . . . not to bandy arguments—no good comes out of that." Dr. Moffatt is not the kind of man to disparage or to discourage the exercise of mental gymnastics, the battle of wits; but he sees in this passage the thought of the futility of most of that habit. Some of us lesser mortals are inclined to wonder whether, in spiritual things, argument ever does any good at all.

One further thing about such words: (3) They can be tragically perilous—"to the ruin of the hearers." All this heat about matters of doubtful importance can have a very serious effect on those "outside the fight," those who are looking on, bewildered, disillusioned; so often they have been undermined, overthrown, and have let go their faith. The word translated "ruin" is the one from which our word "catastrophe" comes; and, in the light of this verse, one is constrained to acknowledge that while, in some circumstances, controversy is necessary and even a plain duty, yet in many cases, and for many people, uncalled-for controversy is very near to catastrophe. If we find ourselves involved in controversy, let us make quite sure that it really is a necessity for truth's sake and not for personal reasons, and, having decided that, then let our words be as "before the Lord." Let me repeat that controversy may become incumbent upon us; but unless it be that, let us eschew it, lest it prove the perilous word that leads to a soul's undoing. Above all, let us beware of the company of the man who really cares little about the right or the wrong of his word, so long as he wins his argument. And now for—

The Pernicious Word

There it is, in verse 17: "Their message will spread like cancer." That raises at once (*a*) *The danger of false teaching.* We shall note (1) What was the form of these "profane and vain babblings"? It was a teaching that "the resurrection is already past." This cult of Gnosticism, whose aberrations from the truth Paul had so constantly encountered in the course of his journeys—most notably, perhaps, at Ephesus, the very place in whose city and neighborhood Timothy was working—admitted the future life of the soul but denied the resurrection of the body. They insisted that the moral renovation, the spiritual resurrection of believers in Christ along the lines of Romans 6:3–5, was the only resurrection to be expected. It was past already, as soon as a man became a believer. And (2) Who were the leaders of this heterodox movement? "Hymenaeus and Philetus" are singled out for mention. We know nothing else of the latter; but there is an earlier instance of the first name in 1 Timothy 1:20, and the likeness of the spiritual atmosphere of the context there to that which we have in our passage almost certainly establishes the identity of the personality. In those First Epistle verses a strange and solemn statement is found—"whom I delivered to Satan that they may learn not to blaspheme": that Satan might have power to afflict their bodies, as, for a quite different reason, he had in the case of Job (2:4–7). For the same cause as we must assume in the instance of Hymenaeus, we find a like punishment is laid upon the sin of physical lapse when the leaders are instructed, in 1 Corinthians 5:5, "to deliver such a one to Satan for the destruction of the flesh, that his spirit may be saved in the day of the Lord Jesus." You see, these Gnostics held that the body is essentially and absolutely evil; that is why, in their view, there can be no resurrection for it. Holding this belief, some treated their body with harshness—by pains, and fastings, and neglects; others treated it with looseness, saying that you could do what you liked with the evil thing, and so they descended to all kinds of physical sin. The most severe measures were adopted, in those first days, to maintain purity of doctrine and purity of life; and this extraordinary power was vested in those church leaders to consign the offenders to Satan's machinations so that, after *moral* lapse, the culprits might through *physical* suffering come back to *spiritual* health again.

Do we not see, then, how appropriate it is to find here a suggestion of (*b*) *The disease of false teaching*? "Like cancer," a *gangrene*, as the Greek word is. False teaching is not an isolated blow; it is an accumulating, growing thing. "They will increase to more ungodliness," more impiety, as our passage says—deeper into error, further into sin. Let us not forget that there is a close connection between what we believe and how we behave. Sometimes the question is asked, Does it matter what we believe? There are several answers to that silly question; one of them is this very fact that, sooner or later, belief is bound to affect behavior. "Shun" it, says Paul, give it a wide berth, as you would a poison or a plague.

A word is added concerning (*c*) *The damage of false teaching*. It will "overthrow the faith of some," in addition to all the other results that have been suggested. There was a time when, in the simplicity and reality of their trust in their Savior, they walked so closely and so happily in the ways of God; but then came those who "twist the Scriptures," not only, as 2 Peter 3:16 says, "to their own destruction," but to the destruction of many another. It isn't merely that their faith in the old doctrine is undermined, but that their faith in the Lord Himself is overthrown.

But let us turn from all this consideration of the pernicious word of false teaching and dwell for a bit, before we pass to the last of our three words, on (*d*) *The domicile of true teaching*. We have here (1) The house itself—"the solid foundation of God stands." That word "foundation" is used with various implications in the New Testament—sometimes it is the Scriptures on which we build, sometimes it is the Master Himself; but I think we may say that in our present passage it is not merely the foundation of the house but the whole house which is intended—the house that He founded. Just as you may speak of, shall we say, a college as somebody's foundation—for example, of Eton as Henry VI's foundation, or of Christ Church, Oxford, as Cardinal Wolsey's foundation—so you have here "the foundation of God," His house and household, the Church, the "great house" of verse 20. And surely it is "solid."

Then we have (2) The inhabitants thereof, as represented in the two-sided "seal" of the building. There was, in those days, a widespread practice of engraving inscriptions over doors—"You shall write them on the doorposts of your house and on your gates" (Deuteronomy 11:20); and on the pillars and foundations—"I will make a pillar in the temple of My God. . . . And I will write on him the name of My God and the name of the city of My God" (Revelation 3:12); "the wall of the city had twelve foundations, and on them the names of the twelve apostles" (Revelation 21:14). Well, these two inscriptions "seal" the house which is His household: First, on the obverse side, Godward—"The Lord knows those who are His." And that "knows" implies that He loves them, cares for them, surrounds them, supplies them, saves them. All this, and all else, is in the thought as in the similar words of the Savior Himself, in John 10:14, "I know My sheep." He knows; He cares—what comfort is this! It may, alas, be the case that those who know us best do not know us as His; perhaps through the cowardice of our silence, perhaps through the inconsistency of our conduct, they have no idea that we are Christians. Yet, in spite of our failings and failures, *He* knows we are His. What an incentive to be and to do better! Then, on the reverse side, manward—"Let everyone who names the name of Christ depart from iniquity." We said some might not recognize us as Christians because of our unchristian behavior, but that is, of course, all wrong. Those who name His name—that is, who are His—should be easily recognized by the holiness of their walk;

they should "depart from iniquity." Attached to the house, as descriptive of its inhabitants, is the two-faced seal—one side says of them, "His"; the other, "Holy." It is for every member of the household to level up consistently to those two qualities.

We have spoken earlier of those who have had the foundations knocked away from under their feet—controversy has subverted some (v. 14), heresy has overthrown others (v. 18); but here is a foundation that abides, that remains unshaken, that "stands." We look upon the difficulties of the world around us; we note with attention the delusions of Satan, for "we are not ignorant of his devices," as 2 Corinthians 2:11 says; we observe with sadness the defections of some—but we rejoice in those who abide undismayed, and unmoved, on the unchanging "foundation of God." David once asked, "If the foundations are destroyed, what can the righteous do?" (Psalm 11:3). Ah, but this foundation won't be—it "stands."

And now it's time we turned to look at that other foundation, that Mr. W. E. Gladstone called "The Impregnable Rock of Holy Scripture"—

The Precious Word

It is seen in verse 15, "the word of truth." Those who remember the great Torrey and Alexander missions in this country will recall how that this verse was a kind of watchword—what we would now call a "slogan" of their campaigns. In sending letters, people would put on the envelopes "2 Timothy 2:15"; they would dispatch telegrams bearing the message "Two Timothy Two Fifteen"; they would greet one another in the street with the same words; there were placards on the construction fences, posters at the houses—everywhere was 2 Timothy 2:15. Well, here it is again: we might very profitably adopt it as the slogan, the motto, of our own life. It seems to me to be a most delightful summing-up of a satisfactory Christian life with a revelation of its secret, "the word of truth."

See here, then (*a*) *The work well done*—"a worker who does not need to be ashamed." This is just another illustration of the strenuousness of the Christian life, which this second chapter has so urgently underlined. We have already learned that the believer is intended to be a soldier, an athlete, and a farmer—now he is an artisan: he is expected to be a worker. Evidently, the Christian life is no picnic! How will this worker become ashamed?

(1) If he does his work badly—we ought all, and always, to put our very best into it; but do we? How often we go to it very ill prepared. A Sunday school teacher, for instance, puts hardly anything into the task of getting his lesson ready, scarcely looks at it until Saturday evening, has got so into the habit of slackness that he has come to feel that almost anything will do for the children. In the day when our Christian work is judged (1 Corinthians 3:11–15), such a man would stand dreadfully ashamed. He had better be thoroughly ashamed of himself now. Look at Jeremiah 48:10 (margin), "Cursed is he who does the work of the Lord negligently."

(2) If he does it easily—with little cost to himself and with no sort of sacrifice. I have heard of Christian people refusing to take up spiritual work offered to them because it would mean giving up some bit of selfish enjoyment, or because they are so shy and would feel so dreadfully nervous, or because they fear they would get very tired. Make no mistake about it that a service without sacrifice is a shameworthy thing. The service that counts is the service that costs. So then, how much does your Christian work cost you?

(3) If he does it fitfully—doing something if he feels like it; dropping it (and leaving the church!) if anyone dares to criticize at all; taking it up again if the inducement is powerful enough, or if the flattery is sufficiently agreeable. What a terrible way to treat what is one of the highest privileges of mankind.

(4) If he does nothing at all—a drone in the hive. A stranger was talking with one of the monks at the St. Bernard Hospice when one of the grand, magnificent dogs came home. It just slinked by, its tail down, its head dejected, its whole bearing the picture of misery. "What's the matter with that dog?" asked the visitor. "Oh, it has found nobody to help, and it is feeling so ashamed." My friends, we could never have that brave animal's excuse—lost on the bleak mountains is a multitude of souls, needing desperately the help that we Christians alone can give; when we come Home at the end of the day, how terribly ashamed we shall be if we have never attempted to do a thing to help them. Some of us Christians are content to remain in our arm chairs, never moving a foot, never stirring a finger, to serve. Any such will have painful cause to hang their heads with shame when we meet the Lord. How grand, though, to be one of those faithful servants of His who have no need to be ashamed.

That leads us to the thought of (*b*) *The Master well pleased*— "Be diligent to present yourself approved to God." This means, (1) As one He can use. Like a worker who comes each morning to his employer's office to present himself for duty, ready for orders—God approves of that attitude. May we thus present ourselves every day—"present your bodies a living sacrifice, holy, acceptable to God, which is your reasonable [logical] service" (Romans 12:1).

(2) As one He can trust. Alas, He cannot always trust all His servants. In all the exquisite reality of His humanity, we hear of Christ leaning upon the sympathy and fellowship of His friends in a time of direst need—"stay here and watch with Me" (Matthew 26:38); but He found He could not rely on them; they went to sleep and let Him down. On the other side of the matter, we shall recall that word the Lord spoke to Elijah, in 1 Kings 17:9, "See, I have commanded a widow woman there to provide for you." Having commanded, He knew He could rely on her to

do it. Mind you, if ever a person would have been justified in saying that she couldn't do it, it was she. There was nothing left in the larder, the last little scraps were about to be used in the last bit of food before she and her boy must give themselves over, in that time of drought and famine, to death from starvation. How could she possibly feed the prophet besides? Was she willing? That was the crux of the matter; for, if she was willing, God would arrange for the doing of it—however impossible it appeared. In all questions of God's service, He asks only for willing obedience—He will see to the means for doing it. How He "approved" of that woman of Zarephath that day, seeing she proved He could absolutely rely on her. And, on us? A poor, ragged little fellow, who had no one to care for him, and who had recently been converted, was asked, "If God loves you, why doesn't He tell somebody to look after you?" To which he rather sadly replied, "I expect He does tell somebody, but somebody forgets." Is that somebody you? Has some poor, sin-stained, needy soul crossed your path, whom God expected you to help, and did you forget—or fail? Oh, to be so in touch with God, day by day, that we may almost instinctively know His mind and do His will and so be "approved to God."

(3) As one He can reward. When life's day is ended and we go into His presence on finishing our job, may we be able to present ourselves "approved . . . not ashamed," and to receive the supernal recompense of His "Well done, good and faithful servant. . . . Enter into the joy of your Lord" (Matthew 25:21). To enjoy His approval and to share His joy: what a rich reward for any pains and sacrifices that our work may have involved. But such an approval will probably mean a considerable curtailment of others-pleasing, and certainly a complete end of self-pleasing.

So we come to a closing thought, one which will supply the secret of this satisfactory Christian life and which has, all this while, been on our minds—the precious word: (c) *The Book well used*—"rightly dividing the word of truth." This word is placed in every "worker's" hand: it is his tool which he must, by much study and practice, learn how to use skillfully, and which he must, on no account, allow to become blunted by misuse or rusty from disuse. He must be, in every sense, a man of the Book. What is this "rightly dividing"? It is one word in the Greek and means "cutting straight." All sorts of suggestions have been made by the commentators. Some refer it to Straight Furrows: the Book is a very fruitful field; to receive its full harvest the plowman cuts his furrows straight. Or, maybe it is Straight Roads: the Book is a great domain; to gain access to its many benefits the engineer cuts his roads straight through. John Calvin has a delightful suggestion. He thinks of Straight Slices: the Book is a wondrous loaf, a Bread of Life; to enjoy its nourishing strength the steward cuts straight slices for his own use and for that of the whole household. Straight furrows, shall we say, of painstaking study; straight roads, perhaps, of dispensational study; straight slices of regular study—not just lumps pulled off the loaf from any part, not isolated texts and bits, torn from their context, to feed some favored theory, but the straight slices of an orderly system—the Scripture Union plan, perhaps, or that of the International Bible Reading Association or the Bible Reading Fellowship, or the Chapter a Day method, or the regular Church Calendar—something like Jehoiachin's "allowance" from Evil-merodach in 2 Kings 25:30, "a portion for each day, all the days of his life." But, perhaps, what we are especially taught here is not so much the importance of the "cutting" as the value of the "straight"—to deal in a straightforward way with the Bible to the exclusion of all fanciful deviations and all "private interpretation" (2 Peter 1:20).

To be "approved to God" we must "study" (A.V.)—or, be "diligent"; above all we must "study . . . the word of truth"— "the Scripture of Truth," to borrow the phrase of Daniel 10:21. Both in our personal life and in our spiritual work, the Bible must have prime place; and we shall soon discover that it is not enough merely to read our daily portion, admirable though that laudable custom is, but we must give ourselves to diligent study—making time and taking pains.

THE VESSELS OF THE HOUSE

2 Timothy 2:20–21

20. But in a great house there are not only vessels of gold and silver, but also of wood and clay, some for honor and some for dishonor.
21. Therefore if anyone cleanses himself from the latter, he will be a vessel for honor, sanctified and useful for the Master, prepared for every good work.

9

THE VESSELS OF THE HOUSE

2 Timothy 2:20–21

O UR apostle sometimes speaks of Christians as members of
the Household, as in Ephesians 2:19: "Now, therefore, you
are no longer strangers and foreigners, but fellow citizens with
the saints and members of the household of God." In our present
passage, however, he thinks of us as vessels of the Household. He
was, we remember, a vessel himself; for, in sending Ananias to
him, in Acts 9:15, the living Lord had said, "He is a chosen vessel
of Mine, to bear My name. . . ." As you might take down a jug
from the dresser and fill it with water to bear to some thirsty
person, so the Lord had taken up Paul and filled him that he
might bear His name, which is Water of Life, to parched and
weary souls. We, too, are such vessels—each in our way, and our
sphere, and our degree; and it is about these vessels of the House
that this writer speaks to Timothy. To begin with, let us see here—

Their Situation—and Its Privilege

Have you noticed how often the Bible is at pains to emphasize what is the attractive environment of those that believe? For
example, in Isaiah 5:1: "A vineyard on a very fruitful hill"—God's
people set amid spiritual surroundings conducive to the produc-
tion of a wondrous harvest. They failed, and only "brought forth
wild grapes"; but that was not the fault of their situation. Or

again, in Psalm 1:3: "He shall be like a tree planted by the rivers of water." A tree must have water, and it is fascinating to see how some kinds—the alder, for instance—if planted away from it, will instinctively push out their roots in the direction of the water, however far off, seeming with their tendrils to be feeling for it, till they find it. And truly by this waterside, near which "the trees of righteousness, the planting of the Lord," as Isaiah 61:3 calls us, are set, there is found all the moisture that will ensure that they shall be fruitful and that their leaf shall not wither. Then, in Psalm 16:6, "The lines have fallen to me in pleasant places; yes, I have a good inheritance." How many have reason to be eternally, and daily, grateful for such—a godly home, a live church, a keen circle, an inspiring friend.

Look at it another way. In Colossians 1:2, we read that Paul writes "to the saints and faithful brethren . . . who are in Colosse"; and, knowing something of the wickedness of the place, we realize how all but impossible it would be to be a "saint" for long in such a place, and how surprising it would be if "brethren" should remain "faithful" for any length of time. Ah, but we have left out what is, indeed, the very secret of blessed continuance in any environment—the words "in Christ." It is because of their inner environment "in Christ" that they are able to stand up to their outer environment "in Colosse." Take an illustration. Suppose yourself to be shipwrecked, alone and doomed, and desirous of sending a message home. You have paper and pencil, and you manage to write a few words; and then you throw it into the sea, hoping (but how stupidly!) that it can live in the water and become washed up on to some beach, whence it shall eventually reach your friends. Why, the writing will quickly be undecipherable and the paper become pulp! Oh, but I forgot to mention that, before throwing the message into the sea, you put it into a bottle and sealed it up. So now, whatever its outer circumstances may be, the bottle will preserve it. Thus it is that "in Christ" they are safe, even "in Colosse."

From every point of view, what a satisfactory situation the believer finds himself in. One more illustration is here in our passage: He is "in a great house"—the Church, "the foundation" which verse 19 spoke of. "Great"—in its spaciousness, embracing believers of all climes and countries, "a great multitude which no one could number" (Revelation 7:9), you and I among them. "Great"—in its wealth, being capable of satisfying the needs of every resident within it, even as it is the beneficiary of "the God of [every kind of] grace" (1 Peter 5:10). "Great"—in its history, having a glorious past, and destined for a glorious future. "Great"—in its fellowship, enjoying within its embrace so many who have had such rich experience of God, which they are so ready, and so happy, to pass on to their fellow inhabitants. "Great"—in its Lord, above all: the Master of the House being our "Wonderful Counselor, Mighty God, Everlasting Father, Prince of Peace," whom Isaiah 9:6 speaks of. Well is it for the house that "the government will be upon His shoulder." To be the humblest vessel in such a house is the highest privilege that life affords.

But we do not forget that all privilege carries responsibility with it. Therefore we stress now that in that "great house" we are expected to be of use. To each of us is allotted a task—not the same task for all, but some task for each. The vessels were not intended to be just beautiful, but useful. Perhaps you have at some time attended a great banquet at the City of London's old Guildhall. In which case you may have got a view of the City's "plate"—exquisitely beautiful, immensely valuable, but serving no useful purpose at the feast, bringing no nourishment or refreshment to any; there to be looked at and admired, not to be, in any practical way, employed. That is not the kind of vessel that we are meant to be; rather are we to be the earnest offerers of Frances Ridley Havergal's familiar prayer—

> *"Oh, use me, Lord, use even me,*
> *Just as Thou wilt, and when, and where."*

Such, then, is the fine situation of these vessels, with the privilege they enjoy, and the responsibility they incur. Now look at—

Their Classification—and Its Challenge

A twofold classification is here brought to our notice; and first, what I shall call (*a*) *A division of personal worth*—"gold and silver; wood and clay." (1) We are reminded of the words in 1 Corinthians 3:12 about building upon the One Foundation "gold, silver, precious stones, wood, hay, straw." There it is speaking of different kinds of work; here, in our passage, it is different kinds of worker. (2) "Gold and silver"—that will be the rich ware of platter and goblet for the dining table; "wood and clay"—that will be the earthenware dish and the wooden pail for the kitchen and scullery. These latter must be contented with their menial tasks; you can't bring them into dining room use. There are some of us Christians whom God cannot employ in higher service— our poor character, our humdrum quality, preclude us from better engagement unless some means be found of changing us completely. (3) What a step-up it would be if we became as silver vessels—yet even this is only second-best. For in 1 Kings 10:21 we are told that "all King Solomon's drinking vessels were of gold, and all the vessels of the House of the Forest . . . were of pure gold; not one was of silver, for this was accounted as nothing in the days of Solomon." So silver is good in its way, good up to a point, but second-best. Let me not, then, urge myself, or you, to strive after that; but instead, as 1 Corinthians 12:31 says, "Earnestly desire the best . . ."—that is not silver, but gold. I am sure we may say that God would have us all to be gold. Yes, but (4) Can this delightful improvement be effected: can "wood" ever hope to be other, or better? Well, look at some interesting and impressive words in Isaiah 60:17: "Instead of bronze I will bring gold, instead of iron I will bring silver, instead of wood, bronze. . . ." Oh, blessed transmutation: that poor wood may move, through bronze and through iron, to silver, and even to gold itself. Notice it says "*I* will" do this: it is beyond our doing. We have just to bring our wooden old selves to His hands and ask Him to make us golden, and He will assuredly find a way of doing it. Let us, then, face up to the challenge which all this brings: Which of these is my true character? Am I satisfied to remain on that lower level? Shall I be prepared, at any cost, to hand myself over to Him for His transforming touch and process? To His very earliest disciples He said (Matthew 4:19), "Follow Me, and I will make you . . ."—they could not do it themselves. What was the secret of Moses' magnificent life? You will find it in 1 Samuel 12:6 (margin): "The Lord . . . made Moses." First He made him safe; then He made him humble; next He made him willing; and so He made him successful. Well might we make the prodigal's prayer our own: "Make me . . ." (Luke 15:19)—yes, one of His hired servants, a fisher of men, a veritable Moses, a vessel of gold.

We have here, also, (*b*) *A division of spiritual contrast*—"some for honor and some for dishonor." I am going here to break away from the customary exposition of these words—with every deference and without being in the least dogmatic. It is generally supposed that the honor mentioned is that of the vessel; but I am proposing to you that it is, more truly, the honor of the Master. Certainly, the former is not altogether absent, for "those who honor Me I will honor," as 1 Samuel 2:30 tells us; but the main thing is not ours but His glory. (1) Some of the vessels are thus "for honor"—they are so clean, so bright, so beautiful, so useful, so valuable that they reflect glory upon Him to whom they are so proud to belong. It was so with this very man who writes the words, for, after describing the revolutionary change that had been wrought by the living Christ in his whole character and conduct, he adds, "And they glorified God in me" (Galatians 1:24). It was the Master, not the vessel, that had the honor. I have often thought what a soul-satisfying epitaph Paul's words would make; if only one could deserve them, what a glorious summing-up of one's life they would be. (2) Some of the vessels, however, are "for dishonor"—a cracked plate, a dirty cup: yes, a certain shame to themselves; who would want to use any such? But what a dishonor to their owner if, perchance, they find their way to his table. And talking about that dirty vessel, don't forget that it is not only the outward uncleanness that is so reprehensible. Remember the Lord's own words to the woeful scribes and Pharisees, in Matthew 23:25, "You cleanse the outside of the cup and dish, but inside . . ."! May we all be "completely clean" (John 13:10). Anything less than this is bound, in some measure, to bring discredit upon Him. Instead of being cracked or unclean vessels, let us seek to be both whole and wholesome, that we may take our places on the good side of this division.

Do you recall the story of the old vessels of the temple: a most fascinating and most instructive story in its spiritual applications. We might call it "A Tale in Three Chapters." (1) *Chapter 1— Dedicated.* "Solomon brought in the things which David his father had dedicated: the silver and the gold and the furnishings" (1 Kings 7:51). It was a great moment; as was that when you, too, were dedicated to the Lord, when you brought yourself—all you are, all you have—and gave yourself over into His hand and prayed Him to take you and make you all that He would have you to be. That day of dedication will always be one of the red-letter days in your life, a day which—if you have loyally stood to it—has always stood out in your memory as one of your chief joys, for "when the burnt offering began, the song of the Lord also began" (2 Chronicles 29:27). But, alas, a sad change comes over the story. (2) *Chapter 2—Desecrated.* First, in captivity, "all the articles from the house of God [Nebuchadnezzar] took to Babylon" (2 Chronicles 36:18). Then, in shame, "they brought the gold vessels that had been taken from the temple of the house of God . . . and the king and his lords, his wives, and his concubines drank from them" (Daniel 5:3). These vessels so happily dedicated to God's service are now so terribly desecrated by His enemies. All too often has that happened in the spiritual history of believers—once so blessed, now so wretched; once so used of God, now so brought into the bondage of sin, and brought down into utter shame. I think of one, as I write—oh, and another—but no, I mustn't go on thinking; it is all too sad. Rather would one turn humbly and prayerfully to the inspired injunction, "Let him who thinks he stands take heed lest he fall" (1 Corinthians 10:12). Well, thank God this isn't the end of the story. The prodigal son, because he is a son, will one day find his way home again. The promise stands: "I will heal their backsliding" (Hosea 14:4). (3) *Chapter 3—Delivered.* "All the articles of gold and silver . . . Sheshbazzar took . . . from Babylon to Jerusalem" (Ezra 1:11). There they are, back in the old place, ready at hand for all the old service—their sad wanderings over, their glad homecoming complete. If any of us are conscious of having strayed from all the keenness of that glorious dedication and all the happiness of those early days of service, may we turn back to Him that we may hereafter be as vessels of gold, bringing honor to His name.

As we go back now to our passage, we feel how natural it is that this father should write thus to his son. Like every father worth the name, he desires the very best for his boy. He would have him the very best kind of vessel; he would have him become the very utmost use to others, and he would have him bring highest honor to the Master. Timothy is a bishop, a leader of others, a man of high position and responsibility in the church—but even he needs the word of warning and exhortation. There is an old saying that "The corruption of the best is the worst," so Satan is

ever cunningly plotting to get the best, and unfortunately he sometimes succeeds. But whether among the bigger fish or among the
lesser fry, we all need to give heed. Yet you will observe that, in
our portion, the apostle is concerned to stress the possibility of
improvement in our level of Christian experience and Christian
service. We may be but wood or clay, we may be dishonoring to
the Master, but these things need not be; this need not be the last
word. There is always the tendency downwards; but whenever
we find ourselves "beginning to sink" (Matthew 14:30), there is
always the ever-ready Hand stretched forth to answer our prayer
and meet our need. So Paul lays his emphasis not on the vessels'
descent to the lower levels but on their ascent to the higher, and
so in his verse 21 he deals with—

Their Elevation—and Its Secret

Look first at (*a*) *The exaltation itself*—"he will be a vessel for
honor"; he had been very different, but that shall all be changed.
Note the implications of this sublime alteration. (1) "Sanctified"—
that is to say, yielded. For the root idea of the word is not holiness but *set apart*, or even *dedicated*; and only in a secondary
sense, holiness—holy, because that is the natural outcome of being
set apart. Put aside, then, for Him, is the thought; but can He do
anything with the said vessel? That brings us to (2) "Useful for
the Master." That cracked plate we talked about, or that dirty
cup, would not be useful for Him; it would be quite unusable for
such a Master. There is a whole lot that He will have to do to us
before He can make us really usable to Himself. Up to a point
He can use anybody, in any condition; God has often used utterly godless men to work out His purposes in the world. We see
that in the Bible as well as in the history of the Christian Church;
but He can never use us to the full, never use us as He wills,
until, and unless, we are made usable. Then (3) "Prepared for
every good work." A preacher accustomed to address large con-

gregations might refuse an invitation to speak to a handful; yet this latter may be a most excellent piece of work. You see, he would be prepared for every *great* work, but not for every *good* work—for good work is sometimes only small work. Philip, the evangelist, has been a vessel of life to multitudes of thirsty souls in the course of the great revival at Samaria, in Acts 8; but when he is required to leave all that and to bear the water to one needy soul, a foreigner passing through the desert, he is just as ready and eager. For him, big work or small work may be alike good work; and he is "prepared" for it either way. Our Master Himself is so ready to spend, and be spent, for the crowds of inquiring folk at Sychar, in John 4; but He has already given Himself unsparingly to bring "living water" to one poor, sinful, famishing woman. Both the Lord and His disciple were "prepared for every good work"—whether it be big or little; whether it be alone or in the limelight. Yes, the vessel that is to be "for honor" must be prepared to be the pitcher for quenching a multitude, or just the "cup of cold water" for one little one that Matthew 10:42 speaks about. In the spiritual significance and application of all this, it is true to say that the vessel which is to be "for honor" must learn to surrender completely its own volition—set apart, usable, ready for anything that comes within the Master's will; anything, anywhere, anytime, any cost! "I say to this one, 'Go,' and he goes; and to another, 'Come,' and he comes; and to my servant 'Do this,' and he does it" (Matthew 8:9). Such is the ideal relationship between Master and vessel; such is the actual relationship to Him of those who have been transmuted into "gold," those who have been exalted to the "honor" class.

So much, then, for the exaltation itself; and now for (*b*) *The explanation thereof*—"Therefore if anyone cleanses himself from the latter." Here is the principle of separation: a not very popular subject, but one that is fundamental to all deeper usefulness. The "sanctified" that we spoke of just now was a separation *to* God;

but part and parcel of that is this "cleanses himself," which is a separation *from* all that is not of God. Whatever you or I may think of the matter, I suggest there can be no question that those whom God has most used in blessing other people are those in whom this "separation from" is an active principle. There are those who do not, in this sense of the word, cleanse themselves from anything—they do everything, go everywhere, exactly as people of the world do. It would not be right to say that God doesn't use such Christians; but it *is* indubitably true that He doesn't use them to the full and as He uses those who are completely separated "all-out" for Him. Such a separation does not mean that a Christian has got to be stand-offish, and aloof, and a bad "mixer." Was ever a man more friendly to all and sundry than "the Man Christ Jesus"? Yet Hebrews 7:26 describes Him as "separate from sinners." He Himself, in the course of His prayer for us, said, "These are *in* the world. . . . They are not *of* the world" (John 17:11,16)—in it, but not of it. Friendly, but free—seems the right attitude; and when we say "friendly" we mean no more than that, for we are not to make a friend of the world: that would, according to James 4:4, be clear enmity against God. Not friends, but friendly; and, with all our friendliness, free of all in them and in their life and behavior which is not of God.

It isn't only sin that we are to purge ourselves from. That is, of course, a quite obvious duty—"Come out from among them and be separate, says the Lord. Do not touch what is unclean," says 2 Corinthians 6:17, adding the positive blessed consequence of such a clean-cut severance: "and I will receive you." There is also to be a separation from, a cleansing from, everything that ministers to self. Recall that advice to runners in the Christian race in Hebrews 12:1: "Let us lay aside every weight. . . ." We have usually looked upon those "weights" as the things in life which, while not in themselves actually wrong, are yet hindrances in running the race; but I am not too sure of this interpretation.

The word for "weight" is a medical word and refers to superfluous flesh; and I am inclined to think that this is a training rule, as if to say "Let us lay aside every ounce of superfluous flesh." That would be most germane to the context, for it is just what an athlete would attempt in his training to do. If I am right in my exegesis here, then we are being exhorted to see that self be reduced to its minimum—*self* being, perhaps, the Christian's biggest problem and greatest hindrance.

One final thought we glean from our passage: It is from "the latter"—literally, "these things"—that we are expected to purge ourselves. What does that little plural pronoun refer to? It seems evident that it is the "wood and clay" and the "dishonor" to which the word points. That is, the second-rate things and people. Let a man decide not to have his company among "the lower classes" of Christians; let him beware of those who are content with anything less than the best, or they will sooner or later drag him down to their poor level. If a man, therefore, by a deliberate, specific, and complete act (such is the force of the Greek verb) cuts himself clean from the life, the company, the habits, the outlook, the behavior of the second-rate, he is well on the way to becoming himself in the first-class, as represented by our word "honor." May this be our aim and, by the Spirit, our attainment.

MEET THREE GROUPS

2 Timothy 2:22–26

22. Flee also youthful lusts; but pursue righteousness, faith, love, peace with those who call on the Lord out of a pure heart.
23. But avoid foolish and ignorant disputes, knowing that they generate strife.
24. And a servant of the Lord must not quarrel but be gentle to all, able to teach, patient,
25. in humility correcting those who are in opposition, if God perhaps will grant them repentance, so that they may know the truth,
26. and that they may come to their senses and escape the snare of the devil, having been taken captive by him to do his will.

10

MEET THREE GROUPS

2 Timothy 2:22–26

FIRST, the "those" of verse 22; then, the "those" of verse 25; and the "they" of verse 26. All Christian workers are likely to meet them. Timothy certainly will in his special position of authority and leadership. What shall be his, and our, attitude and behavior toward them? We begin with—

The Delightful Company of the Real

"Those who call on the Lord out of a pure heart" (v. 22). False teachers, such as those he referred to earlier in the chapter, and those who followed them, would undoubtedly "call" on Him, but not "out of a pure heart." These here, on the other hand, are sincere believers. I expect they were not perfect: they probably had their failings, as they would, in all likelihood, be ready painfully to acknowledge; but God, who reads hearts, knew that in spite of these failures they were truly sincere. Do you recall that poignant post-resurrection scene by the lakeside, when, to match his threefold sleep and his threefold denial, Peter is given the threefold challenge, and how, in answer to the searching examination, the disciple answers, "Lord, You know all things; You know that I love You" (John 21:17)? In spite of my dreadful fall, You know that I do love You! Nobody else would know it, seeing I have treated You so shamefully, but You know! Yes, he was real; and so are these of whom the apostle here speaks. We might pause a moment and search our hearts to see if we have any place in this delightful company. Now, how is Timothy to conduct himself in relation to them? Two things, it appears, are to characterize his behavior: the one, negative, "Flee"; and the other, positive, "Pursue."

He is to (a) *"Flee youthful lusts."* Mark that word (1) "youthful." Timothy is very young for his post; he is only about thirty-six years old: extremely young for the responsibilities resting upon his shoulders and for the leadership that will be expected of him. He will be very much the junior of those "elders" of Ephesus over whom he is to preside. He will have to be very tactful in his approach and in his attitude if he is to be the success, and the blessing, that he will long to be. Those older Christians may, at times, be not too easy—for Paul, even a year ago, in 1 Timothy 4:12, had thought it necessary to warn the young bishop, "Let no one despise your youth." (2) "Lusts"—is not to be restricted to the special meaning that the word bears for us. Sometimes, as in 1 Peter 2:11, it is "fleshly lusts" that are in mind; but the New Testament frequently uses the word in a wider sense, for any strong desire or longing or tendency. The natural proclivities of youth are likely to be of especial danger, even in Christian work, when a young man is set in authority over his elders. The youthful tendency of always wanting one's own way—when the situation may sometimes be best dealt with by giving way. The youthful tendency to desire to be always in evidence—when often the best work is done, even in a leader, in the background; and when it is the worst policy (to put it no higher) to push oneself forward. The youthful tendency to be overfond of novelty in teaching— taking up the latest movement of thought without weighing it overmuch. The youthful tendency to be blind to the other man's point of view—as if there never could be any other reasonable, or respectable, side than that which one has oneself espoused. The youthful tendency to be in too much of a hurry—having no patience to work quietly for the desired end, an end that *must* be and that must be *now*, or sooner! Let me hasten to add that these things are not, by any means, the exclusive propensities of youth. Older folk are, in some cases, just as liable to exhibit such weaknesses; but I think it will be admitted that they are the peculiar property of youth at large—with delightful exceptions. Well, what havoc they might cause in Christian service. So young Timothy is bidden to (3) "Flee" them. But, on second thoughts, is the Christian ever to flee? "Resist the devil and he will flee from you," says James 4:7; he will do the fleeing. Surely, the Christian should never turn his back on the enemy? Isn't that why, in "the whole armor of God" in Ephesians 6:13–18, there is no protection for the back? No, I'm afraid we must give up that notion; for the Roman soldier's "breastplate" was a contraption that covered his whole body, back and front. The truth is that there are times when the only safe, and right, thing to do is to flee. Such is the advice here: that we shall put the greatest possible distance between ourselves and these things which might so easily spoil our influence and ruin our service. Timothy must be on his guard and on the run. Otherwise, he could so quickly jeopardize his ministry.

But all this is negative. On the positive side, he is to (*b*) "*Pursue*." Not on his own account merely, but "with those": he and they adopting this procedure mutually. What, then, shall Timothy be careful to pursue and encourage them to pursue along with him? (1) "Righteousness"—that is, right dealing. Do you think we Christians are always as careful to practice this among our fellows? Whence comes all this criticizing of one another, all this cutting of one another? Don't we sometimes behave in an extraordinary and shocking way to brother Christians? (2) "Faith"—that is, here, faithfulness, fidelity. Do people feel that we are always to be relied upon to keep our word, to do our duty, to do a good turn? Can God trust us? (3) "Love"—without which all else is cold and hard. It is possible to be absolutely correct, if I may say so, dreadfully correct—as correct as a poker, and as cold and hard. What that poker needs is the fire. And what some very orthodox people need is the same thing, fire—the fire of love—to make all their righteousness and faithfulness glow with warmth. Then (4) "Peace"—that is, no friction, untroubled fellowship, no grit in the machinery to spoil its smooth running and its working efficiency. Sometimes, alas, there is friction in the fellowship—between leader and members, between member and member. Sometimes a member complains that another is against him; sometimes it is more widespread, and he says that everybody is against him. In this latter case, the member had better inquire of himself whether it is *he* that is wrong. It may not be so; but it just may be. Like the fond mother who stood on the pavement watching a company of soldiers go by. They were a fine lot of men and marching well. The good lady's son was among them. Presently it dawned on her that something was wrong, and turning to a neighbor, she said, "Look, my Tom is the only one in step!" Well, it may be that you are the one that is wrong. If, honestly, you find it is so, then change step, get right, get in tune with the others, so that there may be nothing to mar the untroubled fellowship. "You should follow *His* steps" (1 Peter 2:21).

Timothy will find this delightful company a great refreshment to him and a great power in the work. And if, by his fleeing and pursuing, he can avoid injuring the fellowship, he will judge it to be infinitely worthwhile, whatever may be the cost to himself. If he is wise, he will spare no pains in the matter, and he will be rewarded by discovering that these negative and positive qualities have combined to win for him the esteem and affection that elders are not normally too ready to give to a youthful leader.

And now we come to—

The Difficult Company of the Rebellious

"Those who are in opposition" (v. 25). We shall be bound to meet, sooner or later, with opposition. Sometimes it will come from outside the church. I do not think we need be unduly alarmed at that; perhaps we should the rather be disturbed if there is no opposition from that quarter. This might mean— might—that there is no real "bite" in our message, not sufficient "drive" in our work to cause any concern to the enemy. I think, however, that Paul is dealing here with the opposition that may arise within the church, which is always the more difficult to tackle. He is seeking to prepare his "son" to meet it, in whatever form it may arise and from whatever direction it may come. What, then, will be the wise course to pursue in the face of opposition—whether, as a matter of fact, it arise either within or without?

First of all, he had better (*a*) *Decline their disputes.* (1) "Avoid foolish and ignorant disputes"—that word "ignorant" is interesting, it means undisciplined. It is the word one would use to designate what we know as an undisciplined child. How difficult such a little person is, how uncomfortable, how unattractive, how unseemly. Well, there are such things as undisciplined questions, that ought never to be put or discussed—prying into hidden matters, probing into things that God has not seen fit to reveal to us. "Profane and vain babblings," he has called them in verse 16. (2) "They generate strife"—and they certainly engender nothing else. Talk and argument can become a very subtle danger. I don't believe it ever gets you anywhere, spiritually; and it so often ministers to bickering and temper—heat without light. You can triumphantly win an argument and yet be quite wrong; you can be somewhat browbeaten, and crestfallen, through being beaten in argument, when all the while you were quite right. Success in argument may depend not at all on accuracy of knowledge, but merely on nimbleness of wit and glibness of tongue. Much better "avoid" it—especially if it be concerned with undisciplined questions. (3) "A servant of the Lord must not quarrel"—there are occasions when he is bound, as Jude 3 tells us, to "contend earnestly for the faith which was once for all delivered to the saints"; but I do not imagine that our writer had that sort of thing in mind at this point. Dr. C. H. Irwin, in his *Universal Commentary*, had a rendering of this which seems to meet the case rather neatly—he has "The servant of the Lord must not be quarrelsome in the way in which he maintains the truth." The quarrelsome partisan can be little help to the cause, and is liable to be a great stumbling block to those who are in opposition. On the other hand, these opposers can themselves be very quarrelsome folk. Wanting to argue not to learn the truth, but only to "get at you," only for argument's sake—like the Irishman who is said to trail his coat for you to trample on, merely because he loves a row! The answer to all that is, Decline—or, in Paul's word, "avoid" any such embroilment.

However, we must (*b*) *Deal with their difficulties.* (1) And to that end, Timothy, like ourselves, is to be "able to teach." Paul has said the same thing in 1 Timothy 3:2 when discussing the qualities necessary to bishops in general; and now he repeats it for the benefit of his young friend in particular. It is one word in the Greek, and the late Bishop Handley Moule has a delightful translation of it—he says he is to be "explanatory." I wonder if we are all explanatory Christians? Are we by word of mouth, as opportunity occurs, and by example of life, explaining to people, even to opposers, the Christian message, the Christian gospel, the Christian way, the Christian life—showing them the truth? It is vastly better to explain than to argue. And (2) Don't forget that he is to be "in humility correcting." There is to be a humble selflessness about it. His aim is to be not to score, but to save. You will remember that when our Lord said, in Matthew 11:29, "I am gentle and lowly in heart," it was in connection with His teaching ministry: "Learn from Me." It is all too possible even for Christian teachers to be self-assertive, self-opinionated, and self-seeking. And if, as in Timothy's case, it is the younger who is to instruct the older, there is all the greater need for gentleness— otherwise, the pupils may so readily take umbrage, and the truth so easily lose value. We are to seek to help the opposers in their difficulties, but we must be careful to do it in the right spirit.

So we are to (c) *Display real sympathy.* After all, why are they in the position of opposers? Were they always such; or is there some sad history behind their present attitude? If we knew all, we might be inclined to cease being restive and annoyed with them; we might become even eager not to snub or to beat them, but to help and to save them. You would sometimes find that this antagonism arises out of a lack of opportunity; they have never had the chance of hearing, still less of understanding, the Christian way. They pick up spurious criticisms in the workshop or office, they swallow it all, and they repeat it parrot-wise. Brought up in almost "heathen" surroundings at home, they simply don't know. Don't get angry with them; get anxious for them, and try, with all the sympathy you can muster, to be "explanatory." Or, maybe their inimical spirit has grown out of some hard and bitter experience of life. Loss, pain, bereavement, failure came, and they blamed God. They have got it all wrong, of course; but do try to let them see that you do care. Sometimes your sympathy will melt their poor cold heart, break up the hard soil, and give you the chance to sow your seed. Again, their hostile attitude may have been born out of the evil effect of a professing Christian's inconsistency. I wonder if we Christians realize how much harm can be done by a careless walk, and how many have been "put off" by our unworthy behavior. I know it is very foolish of them to judge all Christians by the standard of bad ones—as if they would thereafter reject all half-crowns if one day they discovered a bad one; but, foolish or not, the fact is they

do it. In case your opposer was stumbled by such a bad speci-
men, take great pains to show him, in your own person, what a
really good one is like. Above all, don't be impatient with him,
he needs your utmost sympathy. Then there are those whose
animosity is really the fruit of moral defeat. If you could track it
down to its source, you would discover that that is the trouble.
To quiet their accusing conscience they have reared up this barrier of opposition around themselves—they can only feel secure
by pretending that it doesn't matter, and that they don't care,
and that anyhow they don't believe in that old-fashioned non-
sense any longer. No, don't be cross with them; you will never
win them back that way, your superiority will only drive them
further away.

So the apostle gives us two words to guide us in our contacts
with these difficult people. (1) "Gentle." The Psalmist says once
(18:35), "Your gentleness has made me great." What amazed
David was that, although, by reason of his sin, God might have
dealt with him in great anger, He was actually so gentle with
him. An exercise of His power would, indeed, have impressed
him; but the exhibition of His gentleness just astonished him.
Anything that he had subsequently done, anything that he had
come to be, ran back to that, as its source and secret. If only we
would try this quiet quality, we should be surprised how much it
does accomplish. So often it has happened, after the pattern of 1
Kings 19:11–12, that the Lord, who was not in the wind, the
earthquake and the fire, has manifested Himself in the "still, small
voice." Then, in our sympathetic way, let us be gentle with these
rather awkward opposers, remembering always that "gentleness,"
according to Galatians 5:23, is part of "the fruit of the Spirit."
(2) "Patient." The word used means "patient with ill." It is a
medical term. Professor David Smith says it signified "a sufferer
who bore his malady bravely and uncomplainingly." Those up-
sets and irritations caused by these opposers are like unpleasant

symptoms which Timothy is to bear with patience, even to treat with humor. Those he meets will not fail to be impressed as they see his God-controlled response to what they have had to suffer.

And why should Timothy respond so gently and patiently? (1) To elicit a change of attitude. "If God perhaps will grant them repentance"—yes, that is the whole desire and longing of the believer; no matter what the inconvenience, what the trouble, what the suffering, if only these souls can be reached for God. Acts 5:31 tells us that the Lord Jesus Christ was exalted as Prince and Savior "to give repentance . . . and forgiveness"; Acts 11:18 explains that "God . . . granted repentance to life"; while Romans 2:4 reminds us that "the goodness of God leads . . . to repentance." May it be our privilege so to show them this crucified and exalted Christ, so to reflect to them this goodness of God, that they may be brought, through real repentance, to forgiveness and to life. (2) "That they may know the truth"—the repentance must come first, and then this further blessing, which, if we may so translate the word, really implies "the accurate knowledge of the truth." They have never had any knowledge of the truth, or else they have lost what knowledge they had once enjoyed; but now, whether blind from birth or blind from accident, each can say, "Though I was blind, now I see" (John 9:25); or, in the eye-opening experience of another, "Indeed, I said to myself. . . . Indeed, now I know" (2 Kings 5:11, 15). So is the sad, and perhaps obstinate, opposition overcome. How seemingly implacable was the bitter enmity to Christ of this very man who now writes to counsel young Timothy on the best method of dealing with opponents. Then, such utter repentance, root and branch, was granted him by the exalted Prince and Savior on the Damascus road that, as he reveals to us in Galatians 1:23, the churches heard that "he who formerly persecuted us now preaches the faith which he once tried to destroy." Well, such repentance will automatically remove all past opposers out of this difficult company into the third group that this passage speaks of, the people of the last verse of our present portion—

The Desirable Company of the Restored

"That they may come to their senses and escape the snare of the devil" (v. 26). Two blessed experiences are said to have been theirs, the one negative, the other positive. How often Paul presents truth to us from that twofold aspect. (*a*) *They have Escaped from the devil.* (1) "The snare of the devil," he says. How many are all unconsciously ensnared in that trap: they would be greatly surprised, and highly incensed, if they were told they were, and it is only when they try to escape that they become really aware of their imprisonment. How cleverly the devil lures us, working with, and working upon, the thing that fascinates us. Mice don't like traps; but they do like cheese—and there lies the tragedy. There is a passage (James 1:14) where we are given what one might call the physiology of temptation—"each one is tempted, when he is drawn away by his own desires and enticed." That is the way Satan lures us, draws us away: he plays upon our desire, our particular strong leaning or liking—that's the cheese! So he gets us. How did these people of Timothy's get into that undesirable situation? Why, they were just bemused. (2) "That they may come to their senses," says our verse; and the word gives us our clue. It means, to be restored to soberness. The late Dean Alford puts it this way: "These people have, in a state of intoxication, been entrapped; and are enabled, at their awaking sober, to escape." So they come to their senses. One is reminded of the prodigal, in Luke 15:17, who "came to himself." He had not been himself for a long time. Benjamin Disraeli once said of W. E. Gladstone that he was "intoxicated with the exuberance of his own verbosity"; well, the prodigal, it seems, was intoxicated with the exuberance of his own conviviality—he had completely lost himself. But "when he came to himself" he saw his utter folly, and found his way back home again. So he was restored to fellowship; and so these parishioners of Ephesus, these prisoners of Satan, shall be restored—for we turn now from the negative to the positive.

On that side of this desirable picture we observe that (*b*) *They are Embraced by the Lord.* We come here to what is a most difficult problem for the expositor, and I must try my rather unskilled hand upon it. The last phrase of the chapter reads "having been taken captive by him to do his will." Who is this "him," this "his"? Following the A.V., I have refrained from the use of capital letters until we have seen our way to the possible identification of the person, or persons. They are, as a matter of fact, two different words in the Greek; and a no less redoubtable authority than the late Dr. Samuel Green, in his *Handbook to the Grammar of the Greek Testament*, page 282, says, "The two pronouns can hardly refer to the same subject." He himself believes, in company with many other commentators, that the first refers to Satan and the second to God. Conversely, there is another school, and they have the R.V. on their side, who hold that the first word refers right back to "the servant of the Lord," in verse 24, while the second belongs to God. Only a very few consider that both words point to the devil. Now, two considerations give me pause before coming down off the fence. One is Dr. Green's own word "hardly," in which I think I detect the tone of a voice that is not absolutely certain—almost so, but not quite; though hardly likely, it is just possible there may be another view of the matter. Then the late learned Dr. A. T. Robertson, in that massive *Grammar of the Greek New Testament* of his, pages 706 ff., in discussing the use and force of the second of our two words, points out its frequent employment in a repetitive emphatic sense, taking up the former word and stressing it. This is not always the case: we shall presently come across an instance (in 3:9) where the same two words are used as quite obviously referring to two different people; but this does not affect the other use which we have mentioned above. It appears that no rule of grammar would be violated if we made both words relate to one person. And now, bearing all this in mind, I turn to the late Dr. Handley Moule, remembering that he was both an exceptionally competent Greek scholar and also a deeply taught Bible expositor, and I discover that in his *Devotional Commentary*, page 101, in his paraphrastic translation, he makes the words both refer to one person, to God Himself. So, following so admirable a guide here, I am down on this side of the fence! Following upon this decision, (1) "Taken captive by Him" calls for a capital H. And it means that the people in view are released from one captivity only to be embraced in another. 2 Corinthians 10:5 speaks of "bringing every thought into captivity to the obedience of Christ"—in our present study it is not thoughts, but persons, that are thus happily arrested. But how beneficently and magnificently different is this second captivity. The actual word employed means "to catch alive." It is used in only one other place in the New Testament, Luke 5:10, where our Lord promises "From now on you will catch men." That is, "catch them alive." He was addressing professional fishermen; they would catch fish for destruction, but they should catch men for life. Souls will be different from soles. Let it be added that Satan captures for destruction but the Master for life—eternal life. How infinite a privilege it is if we are allowed to catch people for Him. All too often we regard this honor all too lightly and give all too little to its prosecution. C. H. Spurgeon, in his travel notes, says the herons were "standing in the water, still and motionless, as if they were stuffed birds. They will so stand, hour after hour, and never seem to move; and when, at last, a fish goes by, down goes that terrible bill, the fish is captured, and the fisher becomes again as motionless as before." And he adds, "If a bird can continue thus to watch for a little fish, we who are fishers of men ought to be willing to watch long for souls, if by any means we may save them." Yes, indeed. So, through us, or independently of us, He captures souls out of their former bondage, (2) "To do His will"—capital H again, and emphatically this time; for, in contrast to their former experience, their new captivity is to be used to serve His will. Three wills are concerned: their own will had been lost in their sad intoxication; Satan's will had been imposed upon them; now God's will is to be paramount. The little word "to," here, is not part of an infinitive but is the Greek word *eis*, a purposive preposition. Its proper significance is seen if we translate, as we should, "for the purpose of His will." That was the purpose of His enabling us to escape; that was the purpose of His taking us into His embrace—that we should now be devoted to the doing of His will. "Our wills are ours to make them Thine," as the poet says. How all-attractive, how all-embracing is that will of our God and Father. You may remember those lines of Whittier's in his poem "The Common Question":

> *"And so I sometimes think our prayers*
> *Might well be merged in one;*
> *And nest and perch and hearth and church*
> *Repeat, 'Thy will be done.'"*

Well, Timothy, and you my readers, these are three of the groups you will assuredly meet—and that you must assiduously try to help. I think one of my reflections upon our study of this passage will be, How interesting people are, especially from the Christian point of view.

A MIRROR OF LAST DAYS

2 Timothy 3:1–9

1. But know this, that in the last days perilous times will come:
2. For men will be lovers of themselves, lovers of money, boasters, proud, blasphemers, disobedient to parents, unthankful, unholy,
3. unloving, unforgiving, slanderers, without self-control, brutal, despisers of good,
4. traitors, headstrong, haughty, lovers of pleasure rather than lovers of God,
5. having a form of godliness but denying its power. And from such people turn away!
6. For of this sort are those who creep into households and make captives of gullible women loaded down with sins, led away by various lusts,
7. always learning and never able to come to the knowledge of the truth.
8. Now as Jannes and Jambres resisted Moses, so do these also resist the truth: men of corrupt minds, disapproved concerning the faith;
9. but they will progress no further, for their folly will be manifest to all, as theirs also was.

11

A MIRROR OF LAST DAYS

2 Timothy 3:1–9

"In the last days"—what is the period to which the phrase refers? Some say that it describes the whole of this age, from the departure of our Lord Jesus Christ until His return. Others hold that it means only the close of the age, the last times immediately preceding His Coming. Personally, I believe that this latter view is the correct one, and that what we have in this passage is an outline of the deplorable character that will become outstandingly common among men at that time. Yet, these sad characteristics are, alas, not the exclusive property of that last period; for in different ways and degrees they have appeared, and will appear, through the years. So much so that it has often happened in the course of history that life has become so evil, and so like to such verses as these of our present portion, that earnest people have thought, "These that *we* are living in must be the last days." Yet it has passed . . . a certain improvement has been manifested . . . and then another outbreak has occurred; and once more godly folk have wondered. It may, then, be said that while in the intervening years some measure of the picture will from time to time be seen, yet when the end-time really *does* dawn these dread qualities will be greatly widespread and deep-seated as never before. *Any* time, therefore, that in any exaggerated degree exhibits a manifestation of prevalent sin *may* turn out to be, in all solemn truth, "the last days" before the Day of His Appearing. If we find such elements in our present-day life, we are bound to pause for serious reflection concerning this possibility. It may be, or it may not be—it may pass, as have other similar seasons; but we do well to make inquiry.

Some people have said that Paul expected these horrible things and the Return to come immediately, and that circumstances have proved him to be wrong; yet I think we may reply that Paul never said it *would* be immediate but that it *might* be—a very different thing. It is evidently the Lord's intention that each succeeding generation of believers shall remain on the alert: "Watch therefore, for you know neither the day nor the hour . . ." (Matthew 25:13). Let each following age of Christians watch, let each individual Christian watch—for any emphatic recrudescence of evil men might prove to be the predicted sign of "the last days," whose marks so frequently have shown themselves. As our own Cowper has written, in his "Winter Walk at Noon":

> "*The prophets speak of such, and, noting down*
> *The features of the last degenerate times*
> *Exhibit every lineament of these.*"

It was eighteenth-century times that the poet spoke of; his words have equal point for "these" twentieth-century days as we shall presently observe. Timothy was to see some of these things in his time, as the closing words of verse 5 make plain, yet those did not turn out to be "the last days"; we, too, see these things, yet these may not be "the last days"—but they might be! "Watch therefore"—in case. Let us, then, look now into this divinely given mirror of the conditions of the end-time, and note how it discloses—

The Type of People

We observe them here in the mirror, and we cannot but be struck, in not a few instances, by the remarkable resemblances to our own times. Indeed, as we watch, let us beware of any ungodly censoriousness or unhumble superiority—for it may be that even we ourselves personally, individually, Christians though perhaps we be, are not altogether immune from some of these undesirable traits here depicted.

With this personal proviso in mind, we note, first, that (*a*) *Their Behavior is all wrong.* What a catalog of infamy it is. As we mention each particular, I will add Moffatt's translation of the word—lending, as it will do, necessary illumination or correction. (1) "Blasphemers," *abusive.* Dr. Moule renders it "foul-mouthed"—a strong expression for the gentle Bishop to allow himself! But, what a mark of our day is the loose language that abounds in so many quarters—the lying, the swearing, the filth, the blasphemy. (2) "Disobedient to parents." Am I really reading from my Bible, or is it my morning newspaper? Anyhow, on the very day I was studying this portion, *The Times* recorded a speech of Mrs. E. M. Lowe, former Chairman of the London County Council, made on 13th December 1943 in which she says, "We have never had so many parents bringing their girls to the courts . . . said to be out of control." The phrase might, indeed, have come from *The Times* as truly as from Timothy. (3) "Unthankful," *ungrateful.* Oblivious of any goodness of God or man; taking everything for granted. Having no use for God while things go well; using Him only as Someone to blame if things go ill. (4) "Unholy," *irreverent.* This is, alas, one of the prevailing features of these days—scarcely anything is held sacred, hymns are hilariously ridiculed or parodied, even the Bible becomes a medium for what are imagined to be funny stories; and many Christians laugh heartiest. (5) "Unforgiving," *relentless.* This word, which occurs only this once in the New Testament and literally means "without libation," can be understood also as "implacable" or as "truce-breaking"; in order to gain our end, becoming utterly care-less of our bond, our word, our pledge. (6) "Slanderers," *scurril-ous*. How prone we are—yes, even we in the churches—to scan-dal-mongering, backbiting, unkind gossiping; never attempting to find out whether the thing be true or false. Indeed, the truer it is, the more serious it becomes. They have a saying in legal circles, "The greater the truth, the greater the libel." (7) "Without self-control," *dissolute*. A woeful lack of self-control in matters of sex throughout the land is deeply disturbing the more serious think-ers of the day; the laxity of morals, and the alarming increase of venereal disease, are creating immense problems in the minds not only of religious people but of most decent citizens. (8) "Bru-tal," *savage*. While in some quarters there seems to be a growth in kindliness, there is elsewhere an ugly increase in cruelty. In any case, the savage tongue is still as actively at work as ever, inflict-ing wounds that break hearts, blast hopes, and ruin lives. (9) "Traitors," *treacherous*. Undependable; quite prepared to change sides if it seems to be advantageous to do so; having no real con-victions to stick to; having no sense of loyalty to any cause or any person, unless it be self. (10) "Headstrong," *reckless*. Obstinate; having taken the bit in one's teeth, becoming entirely heedless of right, or of others, or of consequences. What a distressing picture the mirror gives back! But there is more yet.

Behind the behavior is the thought. (*b*) *Their Opinion is all wrong*. We shall not find it easy to accept what such people think about any matter. But see here (1) Their opinion of themselves. Three words apply: "Boasters," *boastful*—of what they do, and of what they are; "proud," *haughty*—as if humbler folk were be-neath consideration, even beneath notice; "haughty," *conceited*—eaten up with self-esteem, bloated with self-importance. How forcibly it all reminds us of the Pharisee of Luke 18:10 ff. "I, I, I, I, I"—yes, five times over in two verses. He had the very highest opinion of himself. And, mind you, he had his points. "I fast twice a week"—even though he was, by his Law, required to fast once in the year only, on the Day of Atonement. "I give tithes of all that I possess"—even though he was, by his Law, expected to tithe only certain of his possessions, but he taxed all. Splendid! Ah, but what a spirit of boastfulness. Timothy would be called to meet, and to deal with, some of his blood relations. Indeed, they are not extinct yet!

Look, too, at (2) Their opinion of others. How terribly misguided it can be. For example, as here, "despisers of [the] good." You have heard of Christians who put people off by their inconsistency ("Deliver us from blood guiltiness, O God," Psalm 51:14); and of others who put people off, despite the best intentions in the world, by their blundering tactlessness. But the strange thing is that sometimes people are put off by a Christian's sheer *goodness*! The mere sight of them becomes a rebuke to their ungodliness; sinfulness cannot abide such saintliness—and, if it is only to quiet their conscience, this hatred of the good is born within them. I wonder if, among the "ungodly sinners" of Enoch's day that Jude 15 tells us about, there were some who grew to loathe the lovely character of that dear man who, amid all the base wickedness of those times, "walked with God" (Genesis 5:22, 24). I wonder, too, what—out of their daily intercourse and intimacy—the wicked heart of Judas made of the holy life of Jesus. Did that traitor become a despiser of the good as these "traitors" of our passage did? Maybe; but, in any case, their opinion is of no value; their mind was all awry. How different is the true and loyal believer who can say, as Paul does in 1 Corinthians 2:16, "We have the mind of Christ"—who in everyday practical life, as they simply "trust and obey," so closely "walk with the Lord" that they come to know what His mind would be about things; who are quite sure of His opinion and ever ready to make it theirs. But, in presenting these "men" to us, our passage goes further still.

Down underneath their behavior and their opinion lies that which explains the unsatisfactory condition of both. (*c*) *Their Affection is all wrong.* It is said that they are "unloving," *callous*—husbands and wives, parents and children, brothers and sisters, living under strained relationships. What a tragedy it all is; and how revealing as the source of so much of the wider evil that obtains. Yes, but in the absence of this proper feeling, where is their affection placed? Our passage is clear: they are (1) "Lovers of themselves," *wrapped up in themselves*—and an uncommonly small parcel it will make, I expect. (2) "Lovers of money." Of itself money is no evil thing: it can be a very useful thing and can exercise a very blessed ministry in the world; but, as Paul had told his "son" earlier (1 Timothy 6:10), "the *love* of money is a root of all kinds of evil." (3) "Lovers of pleasure rather than lovers of God." What a wild, mad, feverish rush after pleasure has this modern age seen with multitudes of its people supremely bored if any one night be without its "flicks," or its dance, or its "do" of some sort. Even some Christians are so swept up by the thing that their love of pleasure is beginning to sap their love of God. A certain relaxation of mind and spirit is, in this busy world, not only permissible, but necessary—provided only that it be of the right kind, and in the right proportion, and at the right time; but to set our love upon it is quite a different proposition. It is a dangerous and damaging thing to love unworthy things. A great friend of mine tells of how, on one occasion, while he was immensely enjoying a piece of chocolate, he said to his mother, "Mummie, I do love chocolate," to which his wise mother replied, "But, Dick, you mustn't *love* chocolate." Like it, by all means, but don't love it. This fine quality is to be reserved for things worthier than sweets. Pleasure, money, self—these are to be respected, and to be kept in their proper place, but never to be loved. "Set your mind on things above, not on things on the earth," is the inspired direction to believers through Colossians 3:2. Misplaced affection is, after all, the explanation of so much of the evil living that "the last days," and even these days, display. Such is, alas, the type of people disclosed in this mirror.

And now look again, and see—

Their Kind of Piety

How strange it seems to talk of such a thing as piety in connection with the sort of persons we have been, of necessity, discussing. Dr. Alexander Maclaren sees them as "pagans masquerading as Christians." (*a*) *Religion as a Form*—is what we have in them; "having a form of godliness," as our verse 5 says. In spite of the sinful life they are living, in spite of the wicked state of their hearts, they have retained a certain shell of religiousness. They may go to church still, they may say their prayers still, they may read their Bible still, they may attend their Communion still, they may even teach their class still; but there is no real, vital religion about this outwardly exemplary adherence to the old splendid habits—it is all unreal, only formal. Yes, strangely enough the form is maintained; but (*b*) *Religion as a Force*—is unknown to them; or, if they ever did know it, they have long since become strangers to it, "denying its power." So far as we ourselves individually are concerned, that religion is a farce which is not a force—"useless" is the Bible's own word for it (James 1:26). The "men" of our present passage are notable for the absence of any restraining or constraining religious force in their conduct and character. Their profession is but an outer veneer, an empty shell—like that fine, strong, exquisitely modeled chair that you dare not sit on because the white ants have eaten away all its "inside" and left only the outward form. Their so-called "faith" doesn't "work"—it is a "dead" thing, as James 2:26 tells us. A religion that doesn't influence our lives is a pitiable thing, having short shrift from Scripture. Yet so distinguished a person as Lord

Melbourne is reported to have said, in the course of a debate in the House, "We have come to a pretty pass if religion is going to be allowed to interfere with our ordinary daily lives"—or words to that effect. It is an empty piety that these people profess.

Nevertheless, I am going to venture the opinion that there are far fewer deliberate and conscious hypocrites in the world than we suppose. Most of this ilk would be immensely surprised at the charge. Some of them have known better days, and are tragically unaware that things are changed—like poor Samson, in Judges 16:20, who "did not know that the Lord had departed from him" and fondly imagined that things were "as before, at other times." Or, like that other of whom Hosea 7:9 reports that "aliens have devoured his strength, but he does not know it; yes, gray hairs are here and there on him, yet he does not know it." How infinitely sad it all is—how easily possible for the writer or his reader. Let us not forget to look at ourselves in this mirror, as well as at those who are thus the more prominently exposed.

Well, the apostolic injunction runs, "From such people turn away!"—which means, I suppose, two things. First, that Timothy, as an individual, was studiously to avoid the company of such undesirable people as have been described. Second, that Timothy, as a leader, was carefully to guard the purity of the church, both in respect of doctrine, of practice, and of life—and so to see to the exclusion from membership of all such.

And now we turn to a second big surprise about these men—the first was that any kind of religion should be associated with them; and now comes the unexpected news that there was credited to them a certain missionary zeal, a desire to extend their ranks by winning fresh adherents. It is a plain fact that while heterodoxy is mostly so eager to get others, orthodoxy is so shy or so slothful that it remains too easily content with those already won. My reader, how long ago is it since you made any serious endeavor to "find another, just as Andrew found his brother"?

Turn again to our mirror and observe—

Their Method of Propaganda

You will see at once that they are (*a*) *Masters of cunning*— "who creep into households and make captives of gullible women." (1) "Gullible"—implying a lack of stability. They are not the only ones to be afflicted with this disability; plenty of men are just as weak, but it happens to be women in this case. (2) "Make captives of"—reminds us of that "taken captive" at the end of the previous chapter; only this time it is such a different word in the original—here it is, indeed, a taking prisoner, with all the loss of freedom and comfort which that involves. Their captures are captive indeed. But, why that (3) "Creep"?— there is something sinister, something of cunning, about it. They thus get the women; but where are the men? Ah, that's where the slyness comes in: the men are not at home; perhaps they are at the office, earning the family bread and butter. This afternoon hour is the safest possible time for these unhealthy propagandists to "creep" around the streets, and call at the (4) "Houses" (A.V.)— doorstep propaganda. Have you had them at your doorstep, I wonder? Mormons, Spiritualists, Christadelphians, Jehovah's Witnesses. How assiduous they are. Don't you admire their pertinacity, sometimes even their pugnacity? Does not their fine zeal move you to shame? By comparison with them, we are so many of us so slow and so slothful—yet we have such an infinitely better cause! Timothy here may rest assured that he will find these people ever eager to swell their numbers by gaining new converts; and he will need to exert himself, and to encourage others, to counteract their endeavors. The representatives of the Master will need to formulate their plans for doorstep evangelism, and to go around streets and houses engaging themselves in what some in the Chinese Christian Church call "gossiping the gospel."

But wherein is the secret of these people's success in this method? I imagine it lies in the fact that their visits synchronize with need in the homes they call at; for they are (*b*) *Exploiters of conscience*—"women loaded down with sins, led away by various lusts." The evil things they have done, the evil things they have desired, have become a load upon their mind. How shall they get release? It is at such a juncture that these evil teachers appear upon their doorstep, telling them that they need not worry, that they are all right. Thus do they fulfill the prophet's words, "They have healed the hurt of the daughter of My people slightly, saying, 'Peace, peace!' when there is no peace" (Jeremiah 8:11). Oh, that we might learn to go to their doorsteps with the thorough-healing message of Matthew 11:28, "Come to Me, all you who labor and are heavy laden, and I will give you rest." Those poor women were "always learning and never able to come to the knowledge of the truth"—in their restlessness of mind, ever consumed with religious curiosity yet never arriving at any real knowledge, any clear faith. And they never will until they "learn of Me" as the Master said in that same Matthew passage.

For it is not "the truth" that those district visitors offer on their rounds; rather are they (*c*) *Purveyors of the counterfeit*—"as Jannes and Jambres." (1) Those gentlemen "resisted Moses" by pretending to do the same wonders that he did. Is Pharaoh impressed by that stick becoming a serpent? These court magicians are snake-charmers: their reptile, mesmerized stiff as a rod, shall, on being thrown to the ground, break out into wriggling life. The same as Moses? No; a counterfeit—their "stick" never was a stick. Shall Pharaoh be unduly moved by Moses turning all that Nile water red? His own conjurers can match that trick—fetch them a jug of clear water from somewhere, and lo, the thing is done. Shall frogs come forth at Moses' word? Well, what conjurer worth his salt knows not how to produce rabbits from his hat—or frogs, for that matter? So is Moses discredited again in the royal eyes, for his magicians match Moses at every point—or so it seems. But their powers of counterfeiting have their limits—"lice" are beyond them; performing fleas they might have managed, but not those dreadful little things. They have to admit their defeat, "This is the finger of God" (Exodus 8:19). Their wonders have all been masterpieces of counterfeiting—not legitimate, but legerdemain. There is something particularly apt in introducing the mention of magicians in a letter bound, as 2 Timothy was, for Ephesus, seeing that that city was a very home of magic and abounded in incantations. We recall Acts 19 to remind ourselves of Paul's encountering there the exorcists, "sons of Sceva," who dared to use the holy Name as an incantation, to their own dire misfortune. And in the same chapter the practitioners of this "magic" made a bonfire of their books of incantations as a sign and seal of the reality of their conversion. Without doubt, the Bishop of magic-ridden Ephesus would be intrigued by the mention of those wicked old conjurers of long ago. In like fashion (2) These gentlemen "also resist the truth" by pretending to preach the same gospel as Paul, or as Timothy. In reality it is a counterfeit of the true. It is the same old message, they will say, only couched in more modern terms—the identity is the same, though the dress may be more up-to-date. "So they wrap it up," as Micah 7:3 (A.V.) says.

Well, this has been a depressing study; but it is necessary for us to be thus forewarned and forearmed. All this wrong behavior, and opinion, and affection are to be expected in the perilous atmosphere of "the last days"—all this hollow religiousness, all this subtle and energetic counterfeit. And if we see these things abounding in our day, it may be we are nearer the end-time than we thought; the Master may, in very truth, be on His way. In any case, we will keep a lookout. But is the hope of His Advent only dark and dismal? A thousand times, No! It is characterized by Titus 2:13 as "that happy hope." It has its somber side; but how sunny is its other side. Do you happen to know that exquisite sonnet of Keats on Homer? If you do, you will recall that lovely line—"There is a budding morrow in midnight." For the true believer, the emphasis of His Advent is not black, but bright; not on the midnight, but on the morrow. If our present passage has had to stress the prevailing gloom of the preceding days, let us conclude by remembering the exceeding gladness that lies just on ahead. As Psalm 30:5 assures us, "Weeping may endure for a night, but joy comes in the morning." Even in the prevalent darkness which this mirror of a passage reveals, there is a streak of coming dawn in verse 9, "but they will progress no further"— there is an appointed limit to all this! Then, hurrah for the dawn of that "budding morrow."

BUT—WHAT A DIFFERENCE!

2 Timothy 3:10–13

10. But you have carefully followed my doctrine, manner of life, purpose, faith, longsuffering, love, perseverance,
11. persecutions, afflictions, which happened to me at Antioch, at Iconium, at Lystra—what persecutions I endured. And out of them all the Lord delivered me.
12. Yes, and all who desire to live godly in Christ Jesus will suffer persecution.
13. But evil men and imposters will grow worse and worse, deceiving and being deceived.

12

BUT—WHAT A DIFFERENCE!

2 Timothy 3:10–13

I ALWAYS think of "but" as the corner word of Scripture. As we follow the narrative, we seem to be traversing a certain kind of road until we arrive at this word, and then, for good or ill, we appear to turn a corner. In 2 Kings 5:1, what a sunlit region we find in that grand description of the splendid Naaman —what a man he was; "but . . .": instantly we are around the corner, under an overcast and black sky. In Ephesians 2:1–3 we discover ourselves in a hopeless and helpless condition; "but God . . .": we have turned a corner indeed, where there has suddenly blazed forth upon us an outburst of joy and hope and blessing. In Galatians 5:19–25, we move from the slum to the orchard— "the works of the flesh," how dirty and dilapidated and danger-ous and degraded they look; "but . . ." what a display of "fruit," the very next moment, the first step around the corner, rises be-fore our delighted eyes! Well, here in our present study we turn the corner once more. In the previous passage things have been pretty dreadful—"lovers of money, boasters, proud, blasphem-ers, unholy, unforgiving, slanderers, without self-control, despis-ers of good"—what a lot! "But . . .": look now—"purpose, faith, longsuffering, love, perseverance"—what a difference! At one point, weeds—ugly, rank, poisonous weeds; and just around the corner, flowers—sweetly-scented, exquisitely-formed flowers.

Isn't that just what one would expect? After all, in the former, it is a company of unbelievers that is described; while here it is a believer. And we remember that "the Lord does make a difference between the Egyptians and Israel" (Exodus 11:7)—in that old instance, as in our case: (1) *A difference in fact*—Israel, like ourselves, is under the blood; and (2) *A difference in dealing*—on the ground of the personally applied blood, Israel is dealt with not in judgment but in grace; and (3) *A difference in conduct*—what a contrast in behavior is observable in the different houses: in one, a feast, in the other, a funeral; fearfulness for Egypt, freedom for Israel. So between the believer and the unbeliever there is, in God's reckoning, a fundamental and eternal difference, and that distinction is to be evidenced in daily conduct and personal character. Thus, there is nothing surprising in the change that comes over this narrative at verse 10. But there is something challenging about it: are we different, as different from the others as we ought to be? You will recall the Master's story of the wheat and the tares both growing together, in Matthew 13:30. The trouble was that, though "sons of the wicked one," the tares were in outward appearance and at that stage so like the wheat, "the sons of the kingdom." I have often met with people who, although not really Christians, are yet so Christian in their behavior—so kindly, so unselfish, so sweetly-dispositioned, so upright, so true—so like wheat, but really still tares because they have not been born again, they have not the new heart. There is, alas, another trouble of an opposite sort: that nowadays the wheat is so often so like the tares; those who are Christians thinking, speaking, acting, being just like worldlings: little difference to be seen between them. It is a strange thing to see the tares imitating the wheat; but it is something more than strange to see the wheat apeing the tares. Fortunately, there was nothing of this about our beloved Paul. His was the completely different life; and he was able, in all consistency, to offer to his beloved Timothy—

A Copy for Pattern

It comes as a bit of a shock to find that Paul here starts talking about himself, and that, as it would seem, somewhat boastingly; and this in spite of the fact that "boasters" were among those that he pilloried in verse 2. There are passages in his letters in which the apostle urges upon us the great virtue of proper humility. In Colossians 3:12 he says, "As the elect of God, holy and beloved, put on . . . humbleness of mind." In Romans 12:3 it is, "I say, through the grace given to me, to everyone who is among you, not to think of himself more highly than he ought to think. . . ." Yet this very same man now holds himself up for Timothy's pattern—and this is by no means an isolated instance of this queer characteristic. The late delightful Dr. W. L. Watkinson once published a book, a fascinating book, called *Moral Paradoxes of St. Paul,* in which he has a chapter which he has entitled "In Praise of Boasting." It is a searching examination of the very fact we have been speaking of. Perhaps I may be allowed to take out, as summing up what he says, "The tenth and eleventh chapters of the Second Epistle to the Corinthians appear a very paroxysm of boasting!" Well, read the chapters and see. Or, if you prefer, narrow the inquiry a little; go to the First Epistle and mark the phrases of the tenth verse of the fifteenth chapter—". . . I am what I am . . . I labored more abundantly than they all." Yes, I know; but look again—the seeming boasting is more apparent than real. He says these things, not for self-glorying, but only for God's glory, only that God may be magnified. He attributes everything about him—if there has been any change, any growth, any energy—not to himself but to Him. It is, as the verse says, ". . . grace . . . grace . . . grace." It transpires, then, that there are occasions when we may legitimately and properly talk about ourselves, as, for example, when we are drawn to give our testimony to "what He has done for my soul," as Psalm 66:16 puts it. Only, let us be careful, in that event, that we do so in the right spirit and from the right motive, and along with the right behavior. Paul must, therefore, be acquitted of all desire of vain glory: if any improvement is to be seen in him, it is only by the grace of God. His estimate of his own unaided worth is forever enshrined in that earlier word to Timothy, at the end of which verse he writes, ". . . sinners, of whom I am chief" (1 Timothy 1:15)! So we approach our present passage, "You have carefully followed"— or, as the word implies, "fully followed up, fully traced," as if running over a copy on which to pattern his own life. We know how 1 Peter 2:21 speaks of "Christ . . . leaving us an example, that you should follow His steps." That we fully understand; but Paul dares to speak differently, as in 1 Thessalonians 1:6, "You became followers of us and of the Lord." That is, indeed, a remarkable claim to be able to make—that in following him, they would, ipso facto, be following Christ. Oh that we, you and I, were so Christlike that such a thing might be said concerning us and our influence on other lives. Mark here, now, the details of that copy which Paul offers to Timothy for his pattern.

First we observe (a) *Consistency in living*—that first pair of qualities suggests that idea: "my doctrine, manner of life." As we have seen earlier in our studies, here was a man whose practice coincided with his preaching: what he said in his teaching, he carried out in his behavior. It is not always that such consistency is found among us; alas, we are all too often not what we teach, nor even what we profess. In the days of long ago a pastry-cook sent his boy out early in the morning to sell his pies in the streets. At eight o'clock he started, ringing his bell and crying his wares: Hot pies! Hot pies! It was not a very successful morning, and at twelve o'clock he was still shouting, Hot pies! Hot pies! I suspect that, in spite of his loud profession, his pies had by then lost a good deal of their early warmth. Even as some of us Christians are still protesting our keenness when our hearts have grown cold. So, too, are we sometimes guilty of harboring things in our lives which we have earlier forsworn. Before the War, you might have entered the Hall at Olympia at certain times to be almost deafened by the excited barking of multitudes of dogs of all sorts and shapes and sizes. It was the Kennel Club Show. But on one such occasion, if you are observant, you would have espied at the entrance doors a notice which they had forgotten to take down and which read, "No Dogs Admitted." Yes, that's what it said; but the place was full of them! One recalls the time when Saul professed he had got rid of all the sheep and was answered, "What then is this bleating of the sheep in my ears . . . ?" (1 Samuel 15:14). Pay heed to the apostolic injunction, in Philippians 3:2, "Beware of dogs"; and don't profess "No Dogs" if there are dogs. Or, pursuing our inconsistencies still further, are we careful to live up to the name we bear as Christians, "that noble name by which you are called," as James 2:7 has it? "I haven't a penny to my name," said a man at Barnet County Court the other day. Believe it or not, his name was Cash! Do you recall the scarifying word to Sardis in Revelation 3:1, "You have a name that you are alive, but you are dead." The simple illustrations will, perhaps, serve to pull us up in our infidelities; let them suffice to hold up before our conscience the inconsistency of a cold heart, a sin-ridden life, an unrealized name. Let us, with relief, turn back to our apostle, so utterly consistent in the relationship between lip and life that, as in Philippians 4:9, he can venture on the advice, "The things which you . . . heard [from me] and saw in me, these do." Yes, lip and life exactly coincided. That is one part of this copy.

Next we have (*b*) *Continuance in laboring*—which I think I see in the next three features here: "purpose, faith, longsuffering." There will be no denial that Paul's one great overmastering purpose in life was the all-out, and all-in, service of God. Listen to him on the storm-tossed vessel in Acts 27:23: "God to whom I belong and whom I serve." We may, next, take the "faith" in the sense of fidelity—utter faithfulness to the service which he had undertaken; and the "longsuffering" will indicate something of the price demanded by his fidelity to that purpose to serve. We shall deal a little more explicitly with this cost later in this study. We shall only stay at the point just now to emphasize the contrast between Paul's consuming loyalty and our own all-too-frequently feeble allegiance to God's service. Not a few of us sit far too loosely to our obligations in this sphere. If our Christian work makes us a bit tired, we are all-too-prone to throw it up; if anyone dares to criticize our work, we are quick to resent it (whether they are right or wrong), and as likely as not we resign and "leave the church." All this is no exaggeration, as my readers will very well know. Oh, for more of the purpose, faithfulness, and readiness for cost that characterized Paul's life! This is a second part of his copy.

And the third is (c) *Constancy in loving*—"love, perseverance" are the two last qualities that he mentions here: that is, a love that keeps on loving; putting up with so much but loving just the same. In an earlier war, an officer and his batman, crossing the scene of a recent battle, came upon a badly wounded enemy. Noticing his distress, the officer bade his man give him a drink from his canteen. At that, the sick man feebly managed to get out his revolver, and, too weak to take proper aim, fired at his stooping would-be helper. The shot fortunately went astray, and the man asked, "What shall I do now, sir?" His officer said quietly, "Give him the water just the same." Who could blame those two soldiers if, so greatly provoked, they had left the wounded man to his fate? Yet we remember that according to Romans 5:6–10, it was "when we were still without strength," "while we were still sinners," "when we were enemies," that God, in Christ, dealt so lovingly with us, proffering us "living water" even though we were so regardless of His grace. Paul had learned that lesson, had imbibed that spirit; he would have his Timothy display the same undeviating love even to those who, as the epistle forewarns him, shall presently treat him so badly. "Love never fails," he had taught his Corinthian friends (1 Corinthians 13:8); to Timothy, not in words only but in practical example, he would teach this thing; and we, too, please God, shall pick up the same lesson. So, in these three particulars, this spiritual father has set before his son in the faith this copy of a life good and true, upon which, by the Holy Spirit, the younger man shall model and fashion his own character. Truly, it is a pattern so well worthwhile spending all possible pains on. And now comes—

A Cause for Praise

Paul continues to talk about himself; but, let us stress again not that it shall appear how good and great he is, but how strong and faithful his Savior is. He touches first upon (*a*) *His own experience*—"what persecutions I endured." We soft-living Christians should, I think, read and ponder such a passage as 2 Corinthians 11:23–28: "In labors more abundant, in stripes above measure, in prisons more frequently, in deaths often. From the Jews five times I received forty stripes minus one. Three times I was beaten with rods; once I was stoned; three times I was shipwrecked; a night and a day I have been in the deep; in journeys often, in perils of waters, in perils of robbers, in perils of my own countrymen, in perils of the Gentiles, in perils in the city, in perils in the wilderness, in perils in the sea, in perils among false brethren; in weariness and toil, in sleeplessness often, in hunger and thirst, in fastings often, in cold and nakedness." What a catalog of costs accruing to his allegiance; no wonder he said, in Galatians 6:17, "I bear in my body the marks of the Lord Jesus." How little, by comparison, seem our own inconveniences, and oppositions, and sufferings, and pains for His sake. I notice that Antioch, Iconium and Lystra are mentioned as the places of suffering; because it was the happenings in this particular district that Timothy would be familiar with—stories from the first two cities would reach his own native Lystra, and what took place there, the stoning and so on, would quite likely have transpired under his very own eyes. Thus was he able to "fully trace," as it were with his own finger, the copy of utmost fidelity that, as we have seen, Paul gave him for his pattern. But, in referring to this cluster of cities, why is Derbe left out? A glance at the narrative in Acts 14 reveals the reason—that he was not persecuted in that place. Just one of the multitude of incidental and undesigned coincidences which indicate the extreme accuracy of the Scriptures. It would have been so natural, and so easy, to slip Derbe into the list; but then it would have been inaccurate. Shall I be howled down as a quite hopeless "back number" if I dare to confess that the argument of *Blunt's Scriptural Coincidences* still appeals to me?

Then Paul turns to (*b*) *The common Christian experience*— "yes, and all who desire to live godly in Christ Jesus will suffer persecution." Here we see (1) The intention OF godly living— the "will" is to be stressed, as the indication of a deliberate purpose. Have we made it a specific *d*ecision that, as God's children, we will live godly? (2) The secret of godly living—this will then concern us. It is only "in Christ Jesus" that we can accomplish it. Even as a plant can only live its proper life "in the earth," so we are able to do so only as we abide in Him. Such is His own teaching in John 15:4 ff. (3) The cost of godly living—this must, however, be faced. A godly life will always attract the devil's attention; for it is so powerful an influence that he dare not leave it undisturbed. The persecution may not as in Paul's case take with us the form of physical onslaught; but there will be opposition of some sort—ridicule, ostracism, continual nagging, obstruction, or what not. Even as I prepared this lecture, a letter came to me from a young army officer, in the course of which he wrote, "Do please pray for me. I am having a difficult time just now from opposition." Yes, whether in the forces, or in the office, or in the workshop, or in the home—if we decide to live a godly life, we shall court persecution. In the light of the apostle's statement, is it going too far to suggest that if our Christian life is too easy, perhaps it is not too godly? That may not be wholly or universally true, but it behooves us all to examine ourselves lest it happens to be true of us.

And now at last we come to the cause of praise with which this section of our study was to be concerned. (*c*) *A glad experience for us all*—"out of them all the Lord delivered me." Not "from," you notice—as if we are told we shall not have unpleasant things. The Christian is not necessarily granted immunity from the sufferings of the common human lot: here and there, with one or another, that may be in God's plan for him; but normally he will be subject to the buffetings and batterings of life. Yes, they may *hurt* him, but they will not *harm* him, for "*out of* them all" he shall be delivered. I love to recall this same truth in Daniel 3:17 (A.V.)—"Our God . . . is able to deliver us *from* . . . and He will deliver us *out of.* . . ." He is perfectly well able to prevent them being thrown into the burning fiery furnace if that be His plan; but *they* cannot rely on that, must not expect it. Their business is to go loyally on, fully assured that He most certainly will deliver them "out of," even if not "from." How we may praise God for His wonderful "out of" deliverances: that, by His infinite grace, we shall be brought through life, if not unscarred, at least unsullied. The late learned Professor A. T. Robertson, of Louisville, in his book *The Minister and His Greek New Testament*, has a chapter on "Pictures in Prepositions" which, I think, justifies me in my careful distinction here between "from" and "out of."

And now, in conclusion, see here—

A Call for Pity

In our verse 13 there appears, at first sight, to be no such call; but ponder awhile. First (*a*) *The enemies' progress*—"evil men and imposters will grow worse and worse." Of course they will. It is a perverted progress. We are familiar with *The Pilgrim's Progress*, as Bunyan portrayed it: that is the right sort. But there is "The Rake's Progress," as Hogarth painted it: that is the wrong sort. That is what we have here. There is no standing still in sin; be it never forgotten that always sinning is sinking. There may sometimes seem to be an outward improvement; but there will always be an inward deterioration. Herein lies part of the reason for the persecution here prophesied. Then (*b*) *The enemies' practice*—"deceiving." Here we are, back again with those counterfeiters of the previous section of this chapter. Deception is their stock-in-trade; that is their *modus operandi*. A counterfeit gospel—the "other gospel" of works, against which Paul thunders in Galatians 1:6ff. A counterfeit power—"having begun in the Spirit, are you now being made perfect by the flesh?": thus, in Galatians 3:3, he warns us against deriving our power from the energy of the flesh. A counterfeit goodness—for "Satan himself transforms himself into an angel of light" (2 Corinthians 11:14). Yes, it is deceit upon deceit—"imposters" here means magicians or conjurers, like the gentlemen mentioned in verse 8. But note this (*c*) *The enemies' position*—"being deceived." That is where the call for pity arises: these people, in all their wickedness, are themselves the wretched dupes of the devil. What is to be our attitude towards those who oppose us and even persecute us? Shall we be annoyed with them—wrathfully indignant at their behavior? Well, it depends upon what level of life we are living. If, to adopt the phraseology of 1 Corinthians 3:1, we are "carnal"—that is, Christians living on the world's level—that will inevitably be our reaction; but if we are "spiritual"—Christians living at the Spirit's level—we shall rather have a great pity for them. Listen: "I say to you, love your enemies, bless those who curse you, do good to those who hate you, and pray for those who spitefully use you and persecute you." Infinite pity: let us finish on that note.

A THOROUGHGOING
BIBLE MAN

2 Timothy 3:14–17

14. But as for you, continue in the things which you have learned and been assured of, knowing from whom you have learned them,

15. and that from childhood you have known the Holy Scriptures, which are able to make you wise for salvation through faith which is in Christ Jesus.

16. All Scripture is given by inspiration of God, and is profitable for doctrine, for reproof, for correction, for instruction in righteousness,

17. that the man of God may be complete, thoroughly equipped for every good work.

13

A THOROUGHGOING BIBLE MAN

2 Timothy 3:14–17

IN such an age as this, when there is abroad so much loose thinking, lax living, and lopsided teaching, few things are so important as that Christians should be men and women of the Bible—stayed on it and steeped in it. But then, this was no less the case in Timothy's day. As verse 13 said, "Evil men and imposters will grow worse and worse, deceiving and being deceived"; and, indeed, all over the epistle there are scattered warnings and descriptions of a like sort; making it as essential for him, as for us, to have a real, solid, Bible foundation. We stand, as it were, on the shore with the ocean of life swirling around us: and we find that the undertow of false teaching is so strong, and so subtle, that it behooves us to have our feet firmly set upon the Rock, what W. E. Gladstone called The Impregnable Rock, of Holy Scripture. Paul, therefore, devotes this section of his letter to the urging of his spiritual son to be, in all respects, a thoroughgoing Bible man, even as, through him, the Holy Spirit would urge us also to be the same. Note, then, how the apostle speaks of the Book in relation to the young man.

Its Early Influence

We have (*a*) *The faithful scholar*—"continue in the things which you have learned and been assured of." I think I see here two avenues of spiritual impression. He "learned" the things from someone's lips; he was "assured" of the truth of them by watching their effect in someone's life. How grand it was that whoever was responsible for his upbringing discharged the responsibility by teaching him the things of God, in the Book of God, not only by lip but by life. It was part of the Master's charge against the Pharisees that "they say, and do not do" (Matthew 23:3)—that kind of teaching carries little weight. I remember one occasion on which I was having my hair cut. The tonsorial artist, somewhat too personally, remarked that my hair was getting rather thin and proceeded to recommend a wonderful hair restorer that was warranted to be an infallible remedy for my unfortunate condition. He really was most eloquent. Unluckily for him, I have been blessed (or, is it cursed?) with a sense of humor, and he caught my eye as I looked at him in the mirror—his own head was as bald as an egg! His lotion had obviously been of no use to him, so why should it be to me? I am not altogether to be blamed if I do not take what the preacher does not take himself, if I do not trust what, for all his words, the preacher does not trust. Many years ago a man wrote to the famous Duke of Wellington that he had invented a bulletproof waistcoat; and at a subsequent interview he expatiated most eloquently upon the marvelous properties of his garment. The Iron Duke bade him put it on and examined it most carefully, and then, to give it a test, he sent for a rifleman—but the inventor bolted out of the other door! He seemed, by all his talk, to believe in it; but, quite evidently, his behavior demonstrated that he did not really believe. Alas, alas, for us preachers whose lips are not supported by our lives. It was beautifully otherwise with Timothy's teachers. What, then, is he to do with those "things"? Says the apostle, "Continue in" them:

live in them, abide in them, make your home in them, as the word suggests. To stay within the bounds, within the shelter, within the intimacy, within the blessing, of Bible truth is to be happy indeed; to stray outside is to find oneself quickly in Queer Street, to invite the attention of spiritual and moral footpads, and to lose all that joy that reigns and radiates within. Timothy is to prove himself a faithful scholar not only by learning the things but by living in them.

Then see (*b*) *The fine teachers*—"knowing from whom you have learned them." There is something of a controversy over that "whom": quite a number of the manuscripts make it a singular, but perhaps the greater weight of them has the plural. If the former should be right and the teacher was just one, the reference would probably be to the apostle himself: in the second verse of the second chapter he mentions "the things that you have heard from me." If, as is the more likely, he is thinking of more than one, we shall probably look to that grand pair in 1:5—dear old grannie Lois and beloved mother Eunice. What a godly influence they had exerted upon the life of this boy; with what undying gratitude and affection he would always remember them. Paul was right up on a high pedestal in his estimation; but the pinnacle these two occupied in his mind and heart was, I fancy, even loftier still. What he had "learned" from them—listening to their words and watching their lives—was intrinsically of deepest, eternal importance; but, however that might be, the "things" would always carry weight with him when he recalled the holy, and lovable, personalities that had taught them to him.

Well, look at (*c*) *The first lessons*—"from childhood you have known the Holy Scriptures." They are unusual words that are here rendered "holy scriptures": the word at the beginning of verse 16 is the regular one; but in this verse it is an uncommon phrase that is employed. "Sacred writings," or "sacred letters" — is the idea. It occurs in several places in the New Testament; but the only other occasion on which it is adopted as referring spe-cifically to the Bible is in our Lord's words, in John 5:47, "If you do not believe his writings, how will you believe My words?" His allusion is, of course, to the Pentateuch, the Five Books of Moses—the portion of the Bible that has been more savagely attacked than any other; and, strangely enough, the portion which, so far as our records go, the Master quoted more than any other. As if, long before the attacks began, He would set His own im-primatur upon them. In view of what He said in the verse quoted above, it would seem to behoove us to go very carefully in our handling of "his writings," according to His "words." However, there will be no denial that, in our present portion, Paul is speak-ing of the Old Testament Scriptures when he mentions the sa-cred writings or letters. But I want to suggest that he was think-ing of a particular use of them. This same (unusual) word is also found in Galatians 6:11: "See with what large letters I have writ-ten to you with my own hand!"—it wasn't, as in the A.V., "a large letter"; but it was "large characters" that he used. Do you think it over fanciful to suggest that when Timothy was learning his letters it was the "sacred letters" of the Bible that his teachers used for the purpose? The word "childhood" used here can also mean "infancy," so he was just a wee thing: he couldn't very well have known his Bible in the ordinary way at that tender age; but he could have known its letters. I see one or other of his instruc-tresses, with tiny Tim on her knee—his little finger, following hers, tracing out the characters, thus early coming to know the "feel" of the paper, the "look" of the letters. Then, too, his first stories *were* learned out of the same sacred book. Oh, wise and happy teachers that nurtured and nourished this little opening mind from such a source! Oh, you who have a like privilege, see that you follow a like plan: make the Bible the child's book of letters. We have a whole Bible to teach them from. Well—Timo-thy has thus enjoyed, and is forever to profit by, the early influ-ence of his Bible. Now note—

Its Primary Office

The Bible has many functions to perform, but first and foremost, fundamentally, this: to make plain to sinful men the way of salvation. (*a*) *It deals thus with what is our first need*—"able to make you wise for salvation." Man is just a bundle of needs—physical, mental and spiritual; but his greatest need is for salvation. As Peter, speaking by the Holy Spirit, said in Acts 4:12, ". . . we must be saved." A man under deep conviction once went to the American evangelist Dr. Torrey and told him he wanted to become a Christian. "Well?" said that monosyllabic preacher. "I have a great difficulty," continued the inquirer. "Well?" "You see, I feel sure that if I am to be a Christian, I must give up my business." "Well?" "Well, I must live!" "Why?" He didn't get much change out of the Doctor, did he? But he did get this: that even life itself is not a real necessity—at least, not this present life. Eternal life is the one eternal necessity: "we must be saved." Let us not restrict that word "saved" to the narrow limits of being rescued from hell—it does include that, thank God it does; but it means so much else besides. May it be put this way: It embraces (1) A freeing from sin in all its aspects: deliverance from its guilt, its penalty, its stain, its doom, its power. (2) A fashioning in holiness: the taking of the converted man and transforming him into "the image of His Son," as Romans 8:29 has it. (3) A fellowship in His Church: we are not saved merely for our own satisfaction, to save our own skins; we are, as old General Booth used to love to say, "saved to serve"; and Luke 1:74 justifies him. Moreover, though we are saved as individuals, one by one, we are thereupon brought into the company, the body, the fellowship, that we may each take our place, and our part, in the Church's life, and worship, and adventure, and service. (4) A future in Glory: we are not only saved from hell, but saved to heaven—with all the joys, and blessings, and glories, and activities that that implies and includes. Salvation is not simply a negative blessing but a something so gloriously and thrillingly positive! All which goes to show how infinitely desirable salvation is; but our point at the moment goes further than that—we say that salvation is eternally essential, "we must be saved" or *perish*: dread word, dire alternative! Yet that dark word comes—warning-like— in the midst of the most evangelical verse of all: "For God so loved the world that He gave His only begotten Son, that whoever believes in Him should not perish but have everlasting life," John 3:16. Let the modernistic theologians explain how they entitle themselves to emasculate the implications of that dread word while yet retaining the full content of the other words. While dwelling with wondering amazement upon the love of God, let us not forget the equal truth, the concurrent quality, of the righteousness of God: it is the astonishing accomplishment of the Cross that, with unimpeachable justice, it succeeds in satisfying both these characteristics in its way of salvation. But, in our teaching and preaching, let us not omit that "other side"; let us, in all faithfulness, proclaim the clear alternative—the pardon or the perishing. How arresting is that phrase, in Exodus 34:7, "by no means clearing the guilty," coming as it does in such a beautiful context. The great Scots' preacher Dr. W. M. Clow calls it "the dark line in God's face." However much the idea be disliked by present-day preachers, it is there—still there—in the Scriptures. Oh, "how guilty" we are, and how urgently true it is that "we must be saved." Yes, but how? It is the primary office of the Holy Scriptures to "put us wise" on that—"to make you wise for salvation."

And so (*b*) *It reveals what is the only way of meeting that need*— "in Christ Jesus." Timothy, of course, had only the Old Testament to go on. The earliest of the New Testament books was, I suppose, Paul's 1 Thessalonians, and if we date that at about A.D. 52, it cannot have been extant when Timothy was a little child. Still, if he only had the Old Testament to learn from, the boy had Spirit-taught teachers to instruct him in its meaning—

the two devoted women and the apostle himself. The Old Testament showed him his need of a Savior; and pointed to a Savior that *would* come. His teachers were able to show him that, in the person of the Lord Jesus, that Savior *had* come; and led him to receive Him. It was an interesting example of that remark about the Old Testament that Paul had written years before in Galatians 3:24: "The law was our tutor to bring us to Christ." From that old pedagogue was learned (1) Our duty—that is, what we ought to do and to be, God's ideal and purpose for His children. But then we learn (2) Our failure—the standard was magnificent, but man has failed to reach it; indeed, by deliberate choice, he has preferred a lower, and even an antagonistic, life. The Old Book emphasizes that over and over again; and even more does it teach us, namely, (3) Our weakness—it is not only that we *have* not, but that we *can* not, reach the level of God's ideal; cannot, that is, of ourselves, for one other lesson the Law imparts, (4) Our hope—we ought, we haven't, we can't: we have come to a fine pass! Whatever is to be done? The situation leads us to look for deliverance outside of ourselves; and the Scriptures kindle within us a glowing hope as, by story and by promise, and by type and by prophecy, they point to One who can, and shall, save. Thus does the Law act the tutor, leading us to "Christ in you, the hope of glory" (Colossians 1:27). All which Timothy got from his Bible, beginning from his tenderest years, as his teachers unfolded it.

One other thing is to be included in this saving office of the Holy Scriptures. (*c*) *It shows what is the part that we have to play* —"through faith." God's part is to provide—"God will provide for Himself the lamb" (Genesis 22:8); "Your salvation which You have prepared" (Luke 2:30–31). But if that sacrifice, and that consequent salvation, are to be ours, we have a part to play— "faith," which is the hand of the soul, must be stretched forth to receive. The eternal blessing, with all it contains, is for "as many as received Him" (John 1:12). Now this is contrary to all human thinking; this is not the product of reason but of revelation. If man were set to draw up for himself a plan of salvation, he would almost certainly build up his hope around his own merit, his own works; he would make his "hopes of heaven depend" upon his doing the best he can. His natural instinct will rebel against the thought that "our best is nothing worth" in this matter; it is only by divine revelation that he will discover that "by grace you have been saved through faith . . . not of works, lest anyone should boast" (Ephesians 2:8–9). Rightfully, then, does the Bible discharge its primary office in making us, even as Timothy, "wise for salvation." Cowper, in his "Truth," speaks of a humble cottager who

> *". . . in that charter reads, with sparkling eyes,*
> *Her title to a treasure in the skies."*

We, too, in that same charter of Scripture, are assured of that same treasure—not only for hereafter, but also for here. And now for—

Its Subsequent Ministry

When the Book has brought us to "salvation," it does not then desert us and leave us to our own devices. That "salvation" ushered us into a new life, "having been born again, not of corruptible seed but incorruptible, through the word of God . . . ," says 1 Peter 1:23. From that moment the same Word goes on with us into the new life, to be to us so much that we then need—"*as newborn babes*, desire the pure [unadulterated] milk of the word, that you may grow thereby" (1 Peter 2:2); "You, *young men*, . . . are strong, and the word of God abides in you" (1 John 2:14). Evidently, the Holy Scriptures have a prominent place in the true development of our spiritual life, from juvenility to maturity.

How entirely adequate the Bible is for that task; for (*a*) *It is so remarkably conditioned*—"All scripture is given by inspiration of God." You can adopt, if you wish, the R.V. translation, "Every scripture inspired of God is also . . . ," either rendering is philologically legitimate; and ultimately, they each amount to the same thing. Scholars could be quoted on both sides. (As there seems to me no reason for changing it, I therefore retain the A.V.) Anyhow, it is this "inspiration" which is the secret of the Bible's power and which makes it an utterly unique book. It is no use for people to talk about treating it as any other book: you can't, it isn't *like* any other book, it is quite on its own. What is the nature of this quality? Well, the Bible itself nowhere exactly defines it and is content just to state the fact; and we shall be wise to follow the same course. Still, there are some things that may usefully be said. The five words "given by inspiration of God" are one word in the Greek, *theópneustos*, which means "God-breathed." When *you* speak, your word is "*you*-breathed"—*your* breath, and is conditioned by the shape of your mouth, the set of your lips, the state of your teeth, the size of your throat, the strength of your lungs, and even, in some parts of the globe, by the interference of your nose. All which is a figure—only a figure, remember. God's Word is *God*-breathed, despite coming through human instrumentality, conditioned by the shape and size and sort of the human medium. Whatever inspiration is, it does not abrogate the personality and peculiarity of the channel. It is always God's breath, God's word, but shaped by man's gifts and qualities—Moses and Amos are so utterly different, the style of Paul and John could never be mistaken for one another; yet each of these, and all of them, are but the vehicles of God's voice, God's message. That rather remarkable old book by Dr. L. Gaussen, called *Theopneustia*, puts it this way:

Whether they recite the mysteries of a past more ancient

than the creation, or those of a future more remote than the coming again of the Son of Man, or the eternal counsels of the Most High, or the secret of man's heart, or the deep things of God—whether they describe their own emotions, or relate what they remember, or repeat contemporary narratives, or copy over genealogies, or make extracts from uninspired documents—their writing is inspired, their narratives are directed from above; it is always God who speaks, who relates, who ordains or reveals by their mouth, and who, in order to do this, employs their personality. . . . They give their narratives, their doctrines, or their commandments, "not with the words of man's wisdom, but with the words taught by the Holy Ghost."

Or, to quote the more authoritative words of 2 Peter 1:21: "Prophecy never came by the will of man, but holy men of God spoke as they were moved [borne along, like a ship before the wind] by the Holy Spirit." Here is the fact, however we may explain it, and here is the reason why this Book has such power with men and for men.

Then, too, (b) *It is so widely profitable.* It takes the believer in hand and guides all his footsteps from start to finish. (1) His forward steps—"for doctrine." That is, his teaching: how to go on, how to progress, how to get built up in the Christian faith. He will never make very great strides in the spiritual life unless he gets plenty of Bible doctrine into him. (2) His false steps— "for reproof." The Scripture is ever a true and faithful friend, and will not hesitate to point out our faults. Where necessary, it will unsparingly rake the conscience. Alas, how often we need it, on account of commission and omission. (3) His faltering steps— "for correction." We shall here learn not only how we have gone wrong, but how we may get right. As Psalm 119:9 says, "How can a young man cleanse his way? By taking heed according to Your word." If we are really desirous of the right way, and if we are fully prepared to tread it when we know it, the Book will set us right. "If anyone wants to do His will, he shall know . . ." (John 7:17). (4) His first steps—"for instruction." The word is the one that would be used for the training of a child. As we have already seen in Timothy's case, so is it for every believer: he shall, through this Book, learn his first lessons "in righteousness," in right living. For all these purposes is the Book highly "profitable"—just for the simple reason that it is "given by inspiration of God."

Moreover, (c) *It is so perfectly effective.* By "faith" he became "a child of God"; now he has grown into a "man of God." How beautifully reminiscent is this phrase; what power it has to awaken a longing in our hearts. It may be a big thing to be a man of science, a man of business, a man of parts, a man of the world, a man of letters—oh, but what are these in comparison with being a man of God? In the light of eternal realities, who would not rather be a Moody than a Marconi, a Mary Slessor than a Madame Curie? How hauntingly beautiful is that testimony in 2 Kings 4:9, "Look now, I know that this is a holy man of God who passes by us regularly." Something almost identical was said, in 1 Kings 17:24, about Elijah; but that was after he had raised the dead boy back to life. In Elisha's case, it was before he had done any such thing. It was the simple impression of his holy and kindly behavior that drew this tribute—and that, mark you, from his landlady! They have a rare instinct for discovering the truth about their lodgers, and the Shunammite was no exception. How one yearns that, as one moves in and out among people, the words might be used about oneself! I have been privileged to know a few about whom one would unhesitatingly use the words; but, for the moment, it is oneself that one is concerned about. Of course, I know that the phrase is a kind of official title; but the point is that evidently Elisha lived up to it—he was not only officially "a man of God" but spiritually "a holy man of God."

See now what Paul promises his young "man of God" that

the Bible shall accomplish for him. It is to make him "complete" and also "throughly equipped." The word here translated "complete," *ártios*, is not the usual one, and does not really imply what the English word suggests. Moreover, that rendered "throughly equipped" is the same word except for a certain prepositional prefix, *ex.* I see that the late Dr. E. W. Bullinger has a most illuminating translation—he suggests "fitted" for the first word, and, allowing for the preposition, "fitted out" for the second. He elaborates his ideas (1) by an illustration from the way in which a joint is *fitted* to its socket—moving easily, painlessly, effectively. So, by the healthful ministrations of the Word, shall the "man" be exactly adjusted to his environment and circumstances: things may not always be pleasant, but he will always "fit in," knowing, as Romans 8:28 says, "that all things work together for good to those who love God." (2) A second illustration is from the way in which a ship is *fitted out* for a voyage—all that will be required for the journey is placed on board before the vessel noses her way out from the quayside. So, as the "man" sets forth upon the great ocean of "all good works," he sails with his stored away supplies of the Scriptures—food, sword, mirror, lamp, whatnot: all these will he find his Bible to be. In the precious volume, he is fully stocked for all eventualities of life and service.

Considerations of space have forced us to give but a brief and cursory examination of what is a tremendous subject; but perhaps enough has been said to cause us to be little surprised that Paul, in considering the utmost welfare of his son Timothy, should advise him to become a thoroughgoing Bible man. I will only add, *Et tu quoque!*

PICTURE OF A PREACHER

2 Timothy 4:1–5

1. I charge you therefore before God and the Lord Jesus Christ, who will judge the living and the dead at His appearing and His kingdom:
2. Preach the word! Be ready in season and out of season. Convince, rebuke, exhort, with all longsuffering and teaching.
3. For the time will come when they will not endure sound doctrine, but according to their own desires, because they have itching ears, they will heap up for themselves teachers;
4. and they will turn their ears away from the truth, and be turned aside to fables.
5. But you be watchful in all things, endure afflictions, do the work of an evangelist, fulfill your ministry.

14

PICTURE OF A PREACHER

2 Timothy 4:1–5

I EXPECT you know your *Pilgrim's Progress* and will recall that after Pilgrim has passed through the Wicket Gate, and has thus really become a Christian, the very first thing that happens to him is a visit to Interpreter's House. There is so much for him to learn if he is successfully to pursue his journey. And, again, what is the very first thing that is there shown him? He is taken into a room to look upon a picture that hangs on the wall—it is a picture of a preacher. As if John Bunyan would impress upon the new convert that while he is to become many things, his first responsibility is to be, in some sense, a preacher. Call the presentment up to mind—"eyes lifted to heaven; the best of books in his hand; the law of truth written upon his lips; the world was behind his back; it stood as if it pleaded with men; and a crown of gold did hang over his head." What a picture, what a guide, what an inspiration, to any preacher. He is not to be confined to any special class of people—any Christian, every Christian, is to be a preacher. Bunyan lived in an age which did not hold that. Indeed, it was because, though a layman, he would not quit preaching that he was thrown into prison.

What a pity it is that preaching is held nowadays to be of such slight importance, how sad that there is so widespread a decay in preaching. Of course it is so if sermons are to be clipped to the miserable pittance of time that is allotted to them. Only the other day, a visiting preacher in my own pulpit apologized to me after the service because he had been so long: he had been exactly fifteen minutes. So long! No wonder the life of Christians tends to be so weak and flabby, no wonder the preaching is so largely innocuous—when the things of the soul, the things of eternity, the things of God, are treated with such flippant disrespect. Fortunately, there is one kind of preaching to which we may give plenty of time, namely, the preaching of the life. The famous preacher Dr. Campbell Morgan has four sons, all preachers. The story is told that, on one occasion, the whole of the family was at home when a friend called. They made room for him in the circle around the fireside. There at one end was the Doctor himself; at the other, Mrs. Morgan; in between, the four sons and the friend. Presently, in the course of the conversation, the visitor turned to one of the sons and said, "Howard, who is the best preacher in your family?" All eyes turned in the Doctor's direction, for it would certainly be he that would get the crown! But Howard surprised them all by looking to the opposite corner and saying, as if there could be no second opinion, "Why, Mother, of course!" She was the one member of the family that wasn't a preacher, and she was the best preacher of them all! It reminds one of the advice—the inspired advice—given in 1 Peter 3:1 to Christian wives who want to gain their husbands for Christ, advice which I will venture to paraphrase: "That, if any remain quite unmoved by *preaching-lips*, they may, altogether independently of all such preaching, be won by the *preaching-lives* of their wives." For good or ill, we are all preaching that way—some lives, alas, such poor sermons; some, thank God, such moving sermons. Pause with me one moment, my reader: what sort of preachers are we—you and I? However, it is lip-preaching that our apostle is dealing with in our present passage; and he is, as it were, taking his son Timothy into Mr. Interpreter's house, and showing him a picture of a preacher.

First to be considered is—

The Manual of His Teaching

"Preach the word"—not his own ideas, not the sermons of other preachers, not the topical snippets of the daily newspapers, not the ill-digested scraps of knowledge, a little of which is such a dangerous thing: none of these things, but the Word, is to be his source of truth and instruction. In our last study Timothy was exhorted to be a thoroughgoing Bible man; here his work is to be a thoroughgoing Bible ministry—"the best of Books in his hand."

Note (*a*) *Its diligent use*—"be ready in season and out of season." There is a time to preach—at the appointed place in the service or meeting. Outside of such opportunities there are times when it seems suitable, appropriate, convenient, to speak the Word. Few problems of Christian service are so difficult of solution as the decision about when to speak: we don't want to antagonize people by speaking at the wrong moment, but neither do we want to become so exquisitely tactful that we never speak at all. Sometimes, in waiting for the "convenient time" (Acts 24:25), we may miss the chance altogether—the soul may pass on, or, at least, pass out of our reach. Do you not think it immensely important that we should every morning make it our very serious and earnest prayer that the Master would show us during that day if there is someone crossing our path whom we should speak to for Him, and that, whether it seems "in season, out of season" to us, we may be on the alert, "be ready," to do it.

Then see (*b*) *Its diverse uses*—"convince, rebuke, exhort, with all longsuffering and teaching." We spoke a good deal about these things in a previous lecture, so it will be necessary here only to say a word or two. "Convince" is, as in John 16:8, "convict"— show them they have done wrong; then "rebuke"—show them how wrong they were to do wrong; after that, "exhort"—show them that they must put the wrong right and not do the wrong again. It is with the giving of the Word to them that they are to see these things—not all at once maybe, not without some rebelliousness and opposition; the preacher will have need of "longsuffering" patience in his teaching work. By the way, the word "preach" here does not mean to preach the gospel. That word occurs later in our section; but in this verse it is a more general term. This particular phrase is used in 1 Peter 3:19, where it says that the Savior "went and preached to the spirits in prison," on which we must not base the suggestion that people have another chance of salvation after death. It is not the word for preaching the gospel; the implication is that the Master went to make a pronouncement to those particular "spirits" who died in Noah's time. There is no suggestion of a second chance, either in that passage or anywhere else, that I can see: by the time men reach the beyond "there is a great gulf fixed . . . nor can those from there pass to us" (Luke 16:26). Well, there are many diverse uses of the Word which they who preach it, or who in any way seek to pass it on, will diligently employ. This Word is his manual of teaching. Now see—

The Response of His Congregation

I am afraid that, like many another preacher, this Timothy is going to have many a disappointment, many a heartache, for it seems (*a*) *They will refuse what they need*—(1) "They will not endure sound doctrine"; but that is the very thing they need so badly. Nothing is so calculated to produce a flabby Christian life and character as the absence of spiritual vitamins, the lack of good, solid, sound teaching in the things of God; but they just won't have it, they are bored with it, they will not "endure" it. (2) "They will turn their ears away from the truth"—again a sheer necessity of their spiritual welfare; but the truth may be very unpalatable, very awkward, and so quite unwelcome. There is not much to be expected from a congregation that deals thus with doctrine and with truth—all you *can* expect is the very lowest level of behavior.

On the other hand, (*b*) *They will receive what they like*—not the truth of things, but their own prejudices and preferences will dictate what preaching, and what preachers, are acceptable. (1) "According to their own desires . . . they will heap up for themselves teachers"—teachers "to suit themselves" is Moffatt's rendering; never mind whether their message is truth or not. (2) "They have itching ears"—anything to tickle their own fancies, anything novel and exciting. (3) "Will be turned aside to fables"— myths, as the word is. It is amazing what unbelievers will believe, how many prefer myth to truth. Thank God, in the words of 2 Peter 1:16, "We did not follow cunningly devised fables when we made known to you the power and coming of our Lord Jesus Christ, but were eyewitnesses. . . ." Ah yes, "the law of truth written upon his lips."

It seems a poor lookout for preachers; but let them remember that it is (1) *Not yet like this*—"the time will come"; but things aren't as bad yet. Let Timothy, let every preacher, let every Christian, employ himself faithfully and busily while opportunity remains for getting the Word home. Moreover, it is (2) *Not all like this*. The Master's parable of the soils—that is, the response of the congregation, still remains true. There is much disappointment; but it is not all disappointment. In one part of the congregation the Word sown gets no further than the surface. It might have sunk in if left alone; but as soon as the service was over, people started talking about the weather, or the news, or the hats— such "birds of the air" whisked away the seed. Another section seemed to promise better results; but the sight of a bit of difficulty or opposition quickly showed that there was no real work done. A third company among the hearers were so worldly-minded that even when there did seem some hope, the good was soon choked. All very disappointing! But wait a moment, we haven't finished yet. There was still a fourth class in the congregation which happily proved itself to be good ground: the preacher's work was not all in vain—let him be faithful and he will be sure to be fruitful, somewhere, somewhen, somehow. The response will not be all bad. Look next at—

The Demands of His Work

In Christian service it is what costs most that counts most; and Paul's preacher must give due weight and consideration to that truth. Note in this passage that word (1) *"Longsuffering"*— he will meet with much that will try his patience, he will have a lot to put up with. And (2) *"Be watchful"*—the word really is "be sober-minded"; there is to be an ever constant alertness rather than the slumberous inertness of the drunken; he must ever be on the look-out, with all the strain involved. And (3) *"Endure"*— he will run up against prejudice, and ridicule, and opposition, and, what is hardest to bear of all, blank indifference. No, it's not going to be easy.

Of course there is a type of Christian worker who finds that his accepted task makes little demand upon him. Perhaps he has consented to take up a Sunday school class, but his preparation of the lesson is, week by week, very scanty; he doesn't take the work really seriously; his scholars are not on his heart; he never spends himself in prayer for them; it all costs him practically nothing; he never gets tired through it, though he may perhaps quickly grow tired of it, and give it up. That is the best thing he could do, in the circumstances. The teacher who is to be encouraged to stick to the task is the one who throws his whole self into it, who gets worn out, to whom it means real self-sacrifice. Such a teacher, such a preacher, such a worker, will accomplish something for God.

The really earnest preacher's life is never an easy one. (1) He has his own particular temptations—some specifically arising out of success; others, quite different, coming from failure. Either way, if he is accomplishing anything for God, the devil will be at him. (2) He is the cynosure of many eyes—some who may watch him with love and gratitude, to whom his every word and action are of weight and whom he must not "let down"; others, highly critical, on the lookout for any inconsistency. (3) He has an exacting work to do—it will call out all that is in him, if it is to be effective. Timothy is urged to "make full proof" (A.V.) of his ministry—full proof, yes; for it isn't fool-proof. (4) He carries a heavy responsibility—"they watch out for your souls, as those who must give account," as Hebrews 13:17 says. Don't forget to pray much for your own minister; and, even if he is not perfect, at least remind yourself that "the Lord is with those who uphold my life" (Psalm 54:4), and pray that he may ever have a blessed sense of that Presence. Indeed it is true that if we are to "preach the Word," we must be prepared to face up to the demands of the work and deliberately turn away from everythinɢ that would hinder the freest and fullest exercise of that ministry—yes, "the world was behind his back"; and his "eyes lifted to heaven." But now observe—

The Joy of His Message

It is not all joy. He has stern things to say, sad things, challenging things, accusing things, severe things—yes, but the balance lies on the other side; he has such glad things to say. His main business is to preach the gospel—he is to "do the work of an evangelist." What joy is in that message; what joy he will have in proclaiming it; what joy he will get in seeing its great results. What is the message, the evangel that he is to proclaim? There are few places where it is so succinctly put as in John 3:16, which we were touching on a little while back; look at it again: "For

God so loved the world that He gave His only begotten Son, that whoever believes in Him should not perish but have everlasting life." There is, as has been said, "the gospel in a nutshell."

We must begin by saying that (*a*) *It is bad news*—it implies that, apart from it, we are on the way to "perish." It is no part of the gospel to have a man under the fond delusion that he is a very good sort, and in fine fettle, and that he has only got to go on doing his best and he'll fairly romp home to heaven. It will not do to go to our unconverted friends and confine our message to the delightful truth that it's such a jolly thing to be a Christian, and so on. Some of us have tried that message, and so far as it goes, it is true; but it doesn't go deep enough. It is the kind of thing that, to God's displeasure, will "heal the hurt of the daughter of My people slightly . . . ," as Jeremiah 6:14 and 8:11 record. Rather must the preacher of the Word tell the soul his real condition as in the sight of God, and his real peril as in the light of eternity. If he would awaken a desire for salvation, he must, almost always, first arouse a consciousness of the need of it. I say "almost always" because there are cases which have come to real salvation without any sense of sin: in such, that realization has come afterwards. But even these must *acknowledge* their sinnership although they do not *feel* it. "Perish": yes, it is a dread word, an unpopular word, almost a banished word—but we must begin there.

So quickly, however, we shall discover that (*b*) *It is good news*—the gospel lets us know that (1) God loves—"God so loved"; that (2) God gives—"that He gave His only begotten Son," gave Him up to the death of the cross; that (3) God invites—"that whoever believes in Him," an invitation issued so widespread that anybody, everybody, who wishes may come and rest the whole weight of their trust on Him; that (4) God saves—"have everlasting life." This sinful man who naturally, normally, inevitably, eternally, must "perish" may be gloriously rescued from any such fate. The whole aspect of his eternal future is transfigured, and the whole course of his life here is altered—that, while he remains here, being now "saved" himself, he may henceforth give himself, and spend himself, in passing on the Good News, to the "saving" of others. He is at once, and at all costs, to follow Timothy, and "do the work of an evangelist."

For it may further be said about this glorious gospel, this wonderful evangel, that (c) *It is front-page news*—not to be set down in some quiet, obscure corner of the *News of the World.* The gospel is the outcome of the death and resurrection of the Lord Jesus, and concerning this Paul says in Acts 26:26, "This thing was not done in a corner": then let not the news of it be hidden in a corner, give it front-page prominence. Our verse says "the world": then let the world have it, blazen it forth! When Paul, in Galatians 3:1, says, "before whose eyes Jesus Christ was clearly portrayed among you as crucified," he uses a word, translated "clearly portrayed," whose significance is "openly placarded." The crucified and risen Lord concerns the "world"—then, tell the world! So we have the picture of the preacher again "as if it pleaded with men." And now let us turn to a contemplation of—

The Background of His Life

All this while we have been talking about verses 2–5 of our passage, and we haven't said a word about verse 1. Well, look at it now: it is like the backdrop on the stage, in front of which all the action takes place, in the light of which all the story is to be conceived. See here (a) *A searching scrutiny*—"before God and the Lord Jesus Christ." The exhortation is given, the undertaking is to be discharged, as in His sight. Timothy's ministry is to be exercised, as ours is, not in the light of men's praise or blame, but His. What would the Master do, what will the Master think? That is the touchstone.

There is also here the thought of (b) *A serious examination*—

"who will judge." We Christians should ever remember that, on a certain day in God's diary, we are all to come forward for examination when, for merit or demerit, our service is to be judged. The serious event is partially described for us in 1 Corinthians 3:1–15—one of the passages which all believers should learn by heart. Suffice it here only to notice that upon the sole foundation which is laid, which is Christ Jesus, there are three kinds of builders. One of the things which the examination will reveal will be which class we belong to. (1) Idle builders—"If anyone builds on this foundation": the "if" leaving open the possibility of some people not building at all. They are Christians, because the foundation has been laid—nothing can ever alter that; but they have never done any service for Him, never said a word for Him. (2) Jerry builders—"builds with . . . wood, hay, straw." No one can say that they have done nothing; but it has been pretty poor stuff. Since the foundation was laid they have put in work for Him, but it has been shoddy work: the test of the fire will quickly reveal its true nature and will burn it up. He himself will be saved, because the foundation has been laid; but there remains no result of his life. As we saw earlier in this lecture, it cost him nothing, so now, of course, it avails him nothing. (3) Successful builders— "builds with gold, silver, precious stones." Their work was costly as these; it was, in God's eyes, valuable as these. The fire of testing will not harm this quality of service: gold, silver, precious stones, are all refined, and improved, by fire. And note that "the fire will test each one's work, of what sort it is"—not size, but sort; it is not the quantity but the quality that matters. Let Timothy, let all of us, have the remembrance of this examination always in mind.

Meanwhile, we approach ever nearer (*c*) *A solemn moment*— "His appearing." The word is used in 1:10 of this epistle in connection with His First Advent; here it relates to the Second Coming. The word is "epiphany." In Titus 2:11–13 we find it in both meanings—"appeared . . . appearing": the Epiphany of Grace, and the Epiphany of Glory. Dr. Plummer calls them "the two great limits of the Christian dispensation." For the faithful servant, what a grand and glorious event and experience this will be. The preacher of the word, the proclaimer of the evangel, is advised to have this as the background of his life—that He is patiently watching, that He is presently judging, that He is personally coming: what a background for our service, what an incentive for our service. As with John Bunyan's preacher, "a crown of gold did hang over his head." We shall have much to say about that crown in the next lecture.

AT THE END OF THE ROAD

2 Timothy 4:6–8

6. For I am already being poured out as a drink offering, and the time of my departure is at hand.
7. I have fought the good fight, I have finished the race, I have kept the faith.
8. Finally, there is laid up for me the crown of righteousness, which the Lord, the righteousness Judge, will give to me on that Day, and not to me only but also to all who have loved His appearing.

15

AT THE END OF THE ROAD

2 Timothy 4:6–8

HERE is one of the most familiar passages in the New Testament, and one of the most exhilarating. As he dictates it to his amanuensis, Paul is, in very truth, at the end of the road. He began on the Damascus Road over thirty years ago: that time when, in all his pride and prejudice, he was suddenly, even dramatically, arrested, and humbled to the very dust, and converted, and commissioned. What a day that was! He could never forget it; he never tired of telling the story—three times over we have it within the brief compass of the Acts. How he would have sung our hymn, "O happy day that fixed my choice." I wonder if you, my reader, have a "day"—a definite time of conversion to God, of trusting on Christ, on which you can put your finger and say "That is when it happened"? If so, it will often help to refresh your spirit, and renew your devotion, to go back to it in grateful recollection, and perhaps tell others how "the great transaction" took place. If you can't put your finger on a specific day, never mind, so long as you know you are on the Road. There are many real Christians, treading the Way heavenward, who cannot tell you when they started: they only know that by the grace of God they are on it. Or, rather, on Him; for He said, didn't He, "I am the Way . . ." (John 14:6). For Paul, anyhow, the beginning was so clear and clean-cut; and so now is—

The Close

He is evidently quite conscious that the end is approaching. The "I" here is emphatic; it supplies the reason why Timothy is now, in a particular way, to "be watchful . . . endure . . . do . . . fulfill . . ." as in the previous verse, "for I am already being poured out as a drink offering." Up till now the Ephesian Christians, and Timothy himself, have been able to turn to Paul for comfort and guidance and help; but the apostle is now to be taken from them, so Timothy must brace himself and step into the lead. "Moses My servant is dead. Now therefore, arise, go over this Jordan" (Joshua 1:2); "The spirit of Elijah rests on Elisha" (2 Kings 2:15). Joshua, Elisha—great successors of the great; Timothy is to be another of them.

How does Paul view his end? First (*a*) *As the Offering*—"I am already being poured out." In Philippians 2:17 it had been hypothetical, "if I am being poured out"; now it is actual, "I am already being poured out." The picture is of the drink offering being poured forth, in the Mosaic economy, over the sacrifice, a libation of wine. With Romans 12:1 in mind we can, I think, say that his life has been the sacrifice, the "living sacrifice," and now his death, the outpouring of his blood in martyrdom, is the drink offering, setting the final seal upon the whole burnt offering of his sacrificial life. He was not only ready to suffer but proud to die, for such a Master and for such a cause. It reminds one of Browning's young soldier who came flying from the battlefield to report to Napoleon the victory at Ratisbon. Wounded, but eager, he brought the glad news, and then the Emperor noticed his wounds:

> *"You're wounded!" "Nay," the soldier's pride*
> *Touched to the quick, he said:*
> *"I'm killed, Sire!" And his chief beside,*
> *Smiling the boy fell dead.*

Wounds, he felt, were but second-rate honors: he craved the highest, and must needs give his utmost. So was it with Paul, who longed to go the whole length—not mere wounds, but sheer death.

That is one way that he looks at his coming death. Second (*b*) *As the Departure*—the "unloosing," as the word literally means. This is a most interesting word, and most illuminating. It may be said to have at least five connotations, each of them throwing a floodlight on death. (1) It is a prisoner's word—meaning his "release." What especial comfort that would bring to Paul, shut up as he is in that foul Roman dungeon: he is about to be let loose. It carries that thought also to us who are imprisoned within this mortal body, and who that day will be set free from all its restrictions and disabilities. (2) It is a farmer's word—and would signify the "unyoking" of an ox when its long hard day's work was done. Paul had plowed a toilsome furrow all through his life's long day, and now comes rest. A thing that we too shall greatly esteem if our life has been strenuously occupied in God's service. (3) It is a warrior's word—the encampment has been pitched here, and a fierce battle joined; now that is victoriously over, he strikes his tent, "unloosing" its cords and stakes, and is on the march again to the last great conquest of the campaign. How true of the battle-scarred old veteran who pens the words, and of all who follow in his steps. (4) It is a seaman's word—and would be used for the "unmooring" of a ship that has been tied up to the quayside and which must now put to sea again. In Paul's case, and in ours, it is the setting sail upon the ocean of our last voyage, our vessel Homeward bound. (5) It is a philosopher's word—suggesting the "unraveling" of a knotty problem. How many puzzles have agitated our minds and disturbed our hearts while we have pondered upon our life here and its mysteries; "but then I shall know just as I also am known," as Paul himself said in 1 Corinthians 13:12. How utterly grand to have all our questions satisfyingly answered. Well now, our "departure" implies all this—

and more, much more, besides. It is true, of course, that death is an intensely solemn thing—that comes out in Paul's first figure of the "outpouring"; but, looked at in this second way, it is an unimaginably glorious thing. It would appear to be no exaggeration to say that, for the believer, the very best thing that can happen to him is to die. In fact, now I come to think of it, Paul himself says that very thing in Philippians 1:23, ". . . to depart and be with Christ . . . is far better." For ourselves, let us not be anything else than happy in the thought of our departure. Of course, if the Lord were to come first, we should not have to pass through the grave at all, "we who are alive . . . shall be caught up . . . to meet the Lord in the air," as 1 Thessalonians 4:17 says — no death, no coffin, no grave, no tombstone, no epitaph! But even if we do die, let us look on it as our "departure," and rejoice accordingly. Sadness, perhaps, for loved ones left behind to miss us, but for ourselves only gladness. Paul reminds his son Timothy that his time for that is "at hand." It is only natural that he should, at that point, turn retrospectively to look at the days that are past; and so, next he speaks of—

The Course

Here, once again, the heart of the old sportsman peeps out: he turns to the field of athletics, as he has so often done, for illustrations of his life. If he had lived in modern times, I am sure he would have been, like myself, a member of the Surrey County Cricket Club; and if I had chanced to sit near him in the pavilion at the Oval, I feel certain I should have found him, every now and then, making a note on the back of an old envelope as he saw something in the game that he could use to enforce a spiritual truth. We preachers would be much more interesting and impressive if we were more alert to see, in common happenings and things, pictures of deeper concerns. Paul was expert at that; and first it is (*a*) *The Wrestling*—"I have fought the good fight." Most of the scholars think that it is this that he is referring to here rather than to soldiering. When he uses that word "good," I do not imagine he means that he has fought well but that it has been a well-worthwhile fight, a struggle that called forth a man's worthiest and best. There are some causes that we would scorn to take our coats off for; but the cause of God is great enough, and "good" enough, for us all, and for our all. What a wrestle his whole life had been! Constantly he had wrestled with circumstances—hardship, and loss, and suffering, and shipwreck; but "in all these things we are more than conquerors," he avers in Romans 8:37. If only we also could learn "through Him" to triumph over our circumstances, what a difference it would make —both to our experience and to our influence. How, too, he had wrestled with enemies—they had dogged him at every step, plotting against his very life; but at every turn he had proved victorious. If you had spoken with him about his struggles, I am sure he would have referred you to a deeper antagonism, even as he had reminded the Ephesians (6:12) that "we do not wrestle against flesh and blood, but against principalities, against powers, against the rulers of the darkness of this age, against spiritual hosts of wickedness in the heavenly places." When a believer is "all-out" for God, he is bound, sooner or later, to have to do battle with evil powers. For Paul, the fight was now done.

For further illustration he turns to (*b*) *The Racing*—"I have finished the race." The race track had provided him with many a lesson. One of the completest New Testament references is that in Hebrews 12:1, which, though it is the fashion now to hold as not written by him, is yet so thoroughly Pauline in tone and expression: "Therefore we also, since we are surrounded by so great a cloud of witnesses, let us lay aside every weight, and the sin which so easily ensnares us, and let us run with endurance the race that is set before us, looking unto Jesus. . . ." Quite a number of tips are offered us.

(1) Keep the weight down—for "weight" in this verse is, as we indicated in an earlier lecture, a medical term, and the phrase would seem to say, "let us get rid of every ounce of superfluous flesh," which is just what an athlete would try to do. Its spiritual significance is, of course, that we should become smaller—less and less of self!

(2) Keep the limbs free—"the sin which so easily ensnares us," which does so closely wrap us around, as it means, like some impeding garment that gets in the way of free movement. You can't run in an overcoat. Well, yes, you can; I have done it myself—and then I missed it! But you can't run well—and it is good running that the Bible is concerned with; it is not interested in mere jogging. How many Christians are slowed down in the race because of some besetting sin that clings to them; they never will be able to run all-out until they have learned to throw this off.

(3) Keep the eyes right—"looking unto Jesus." It is strange how important the eyes are in athletic affairs: boxing, cricket, golf, and so many others; and even in racing. I think, with sadness, of the silver cup that isn't on my study mantelpiece! It ought to have been; but, leading near the tape, I heard someone coming up fast behind me, and foolishly I turned my head to get a glimpse of my antagonist. In that split second he flashed by. If only I had kept my eyes right! Now I have left only the pathetic picture of the cup that isn't there! Proverbs 4:25 is a fine piece of advice for the Christian race: "Let your eyes look straight ahead, and your eyelids look right before you." Never mind about other people. Peter asks in John 21:21, "But Lord, what about this man?" and gets his Master's answer, "What is that to you? You follow Me." Eyes off all other people: eyes on Him, "the author and finisher of our faith," who was at the start of our race and now waits at the end of it, watching for us to come in—eyes on Him.

(4) Keep the race going—"run with endurance." As we saw in an earlier lecture, this is not a sprint but a long-distance race, and we are to go on and on, plodding along the track, yard after yard, year after year. "Let us go on . . . ," says Hebrews 6:1. Paul had now been at it for more than thirty years and will not finally cease until he breasts the tape. In his charge to the very Ephesians over whom Timothy had the oversight, he had said, in Acts 20:24, ". . . that I may finish my race with joy"; and now he is almost home. It has been, as it will be for us all who would be "God's athletes," a set course—for God Himself has chosen our path and marked out the way wherein we shall go; it is, as we have said, a long course—whose finish may be yet far off, but may be just around the bend; it is a strenuous course—with plenty of opposition and an abundance of difficulties: it may indeed, for that very reason, be thought of as something of an obstacle race. Such is "the race that is set before us." Paul had so magnificently sped along the whole length and will at any moment now triumphantly finish; and out of all his experience this old athlete would say to those who are following on the same track, to Timothy and to all others, what he counseled the Corinthian believers (1 Corinthians 9:24), "Run in such a way that you may obtain it." There is a prize to be won, of which we shall speak presently.

But first there is a third illustration of the truly successful Christian life, (c) *The Safeguarding*—"I have kept the faith." It is as if some valuable thing had been entrusted to your care for delivery to someone on the other side of the world. You had it carefully wrapped and secretly strapped about your person; you met professional thieves on the ship going across, you encountered fierce robbers on the roads; but you managed to keep your treasure intact and at last, with utmost relief and joy, you arrived at your destination and handed the thing over to the one to whom it belonged. So, as Jude 3 has it, "Contend earnestly for the faith which was once for all delivered to the saints." Paul had done that preeminently. On his journey he has frequently been, as he says in 2 Corinthians 11:26, "in perils of robbers," who in the spiritual sense as well as in the material have sought to despoil him of his treasure and to damage his "trust"; but now he is at the end of the voyage and is able thankfully to deliver up his treasure, to hand it on, unmarred. In 3:8, he had told Timothy about those who were "disapproved concerning the faith." He is thankful beyond measure that it has been so different in his own case; for here, we repeat, is no wrongful boasting—as we have previously noted with regard to 1 Corinthians 15:10, he would ascribe all that he might have become, all that he had ever done, to the mighty "grace" of God. He has seen that, as his spur and secret, all along the course of his eventful life, and now he comes to—

The Crown

At the conclusion of our last study we promised that we would have much to say about the crown; and here it is, discussed in some detail in this eighth verse of our present passage. And first we will take note of what I shall describe as (*a*) *The display of the prizes*—"Finally, there is laid up for me." At the Greek Games, of which Paul is still thinking, there would be displayed, in some public spot, the prizes to be awarded to the successful entrants—spectators and competitors alike might view them, in the one case with interest, in the other with hope. They would not be silver cups, as with us, but only wreaths of pine or laurel; yet what high value was set upon acquiring them. Not only were the athletes themselves honored but even the cities from which they came; when the conquering hero returned home with his wreathed crown, there was given him a procession and a reception. I remember visiting a certain school on Sports Day and walking with my young friend around the field before any of the events had begun. Up in one corner was a tent, outside which was a policeman. On going inside, we found a second constable. Ah, but, you see, on a table were set out the prizes for that afternoon's competitions—and these guardians of the law were responsible for their safety. There were the prizes safely "laid up"—for whom? Well, I can only say that my young friend pointed out one cup to me, with its little card attached, and said, "That's what I'm after!" I am happy to relate that he got it. My point here is that there it was, safely "laid up" for him until the time of his receiving it. Thus is there also laid up, and with infallible security, the rewards in heaven for all who "run well." We cannot see them with the eyes of flesh; but our hearts can joyfully and thankfully contemplate this "goodness, which You have laid up for those who fear You," as Psalm 31:19 says. I know there are some high-minded Christians who think nothing of rewards, who just "do right, because 'tis right." But I am bound to confess that, like Paul (alas, it is the only thing in which I can claim to resemble him) I covet any reward that God's grace can, of His goodness, devise for so ordinary a performer. I should frankly rejoice if I could think that there is any reward "laid up for me."

Now let us consider (*b*) *The character of the prizes*—"a crown of righteousness." I suppose we shall be right in saying two things about these prizes: (1) They are for righteous people—those who have the "imputed" righteousness of Christ, that is to say, all true believers. If we are not Christians, we have not even entered the race and are certainly not entitled to the prize. (2) They are for righteous lives—those who, having first become Christians "through faith in Christ Jesus," then devote what remains of their lives to His service and His honor. Moffatt's translation of the phrase puts it, I think, exactly: he has "the crown of a good life." To have life—is not a reward for our merit, but a gift of God's grace; to live good lives—is to be eligible for a reward. Yet even this is not strictly a reward for our earning; if we do well, we have not really become entitled to reward: "When you have done all those things which you are commanded, say, 'We are unprofitable servants. We have done what was our duty to do'" (Luke 17:10). I so well remember, many years ago, being appointed to supervise the "Little Its" race at a Children's Special Service Mission birthday event. I gave the wee people their handicaps—all, of course, sheer guesswork; and one delectable dumpling I placed well in front of the rest, for she could only toddle—or waddle. I then explained the rules, and gave the word "Go!" I greatly hope that the Governing Body of the Athletic Association will not, at this distance of time, declare the decision of the race void when I confess that, besides being the starter, I also myself ran with the competitors—running backwards in front of my little friend, luring her on to catch me! The result was that she won the race, although she was really too young to realize what was happening. Surprised by all the clapping and cheering, she looked up at me and said, "What has me done?" Ah, my friend, if, at the end of the race, you receive the plaudits of the Master and a prize at His hands, I know that you will say, "But, Lord, what have I done?" You will realize that you haven't deserved, or earned, a prize and will only be amazedly thankful that, in spite of that, He has awarded you one.

Think, just a moment, of (*c*) *The Giver of the prizes*—"the Lord, the righteous judge." You see, Paul has had, and will have, to appear before Nero, the unrighteous judge—he knows, to his bitter cost, what that means; he is not unprepared to receive at his unjust hands the sentence of a cruel death. But he has a reward to look forward to that he is to receive at the hands of another—a Judge inescapably just, almost unbelievably generous. Don't you think it makes some subtle difference, at any prize distribution function, who gives them away? There are some people we could all name from whose hands it would be an added honor to get our prize. But what shall be said of our being rewarded by the wonderful wounded hands of the living Lord?

Now come to (*d*) *The day of the prizes*—"on that Day." When we were dealing with 2:5 and the word "crowned," we called attention to "the prize of the upward call" in Philippians 3:14— the ceremony at the end of the Games of being called to go upward to the rostrum to receive the prizes. An illustration of "that Day," referred to again in our present passage, when we shall be called up, "caught up," as 1 Thessalonians 4:17 has it, for one thing, for those who have won prizes to get them. What a grand day is any Prize Day; but was any such like this one that is to be? What a thrill to see the famous veterans of the track file up to get their crowns; yes, and what a thrill to see all the humbler runners, too. What a tragedy if, readers and writer, any of us should be missing from that list—arriving in heaven, because that doesn't depend on the quality of our running; but no reward. A place; but no prize.

Well, look lastly at (*e*) *The winners of the prizes*—"not . . . me only but . . . all who haved loved His appearing." Why so? Because, if we have set our heart on His appearing, it will so affect our Christian life and service that we shall qualify for the prizes He will then distribute; the thought of meeting Him will put that something extra into our wrestling, our racing, and our safeguarding which will render them so successful as to be rewarded. So it is pertinent to inquire, Are we thus eagerly looking forward to His return? The great and profound scholar Dr. Alfred Plummer has written: "Are our hearts longing for Christ's return? Or, are we dreading it, because we know that we are not fit to meet Him, and are making no attempt to become so?" It is a very solemn, and important, question; and it is very evident from our verse that "prize, or no prize" depends upon our answer.

And now, enough about prizes. As I have indicated, I set great store upon them. I am not going to be so foolish as to affect to despise what the Master, and the Scriptures, speak about so much; I am not going to attempt to be so superior to Paul as to think lightly of what he thought of so highly. Yes; and yes, again. But I

want to finish on another note. Do you remember those lines of
the old hymn—

> *"The bride eyes not her garment,*
> *But her dear bridegroom's face.*
> *I will not gaze at glory,*
> *But on my King of grace.*
> *Not at the crown He giveth,*
> *But on His piercèd hand:*
> *The Lamb is all the glory*
> *Of Immanuel's land."*

After all, no "*It*" will utterly satisfy in "that Day," however beautiful and however wonderful it may be—no, no *It*; but only *He*.
So our last word from the passage is not of the Prize and its arrival,
but of the Person and "His appearing." I don't think I can write
any more about that: I just want to put down my pen—and
think, and pray. Will you join me?

SNAPSHOTS OF SIX SOLDIERS

2 Timothy 4:9–12

9. Be diligent to come to me quickly;
10. for Demas has forsaken me, having loved this present world, and has departed for Thessalonica—Crescens for Galatia, Titus for Dalmatia.
11. Only Luke is with me. Get Mark and bring him with you, for he is useful to me for ministry.
12. And Tychicus I have sent to Ephesus.

16

SNAPSHOTS OF SIX SOLDIERS

2 Timothy 4:9–12

THE old warrior has now definitely retired and has here been writing to his young fellow soldier—a word he actually uses of Archippus in Philemon 2—exhorting him to acquit himself well in warfare: "Endure hardship as a good soldier of Jesus Christ" (2:3). And now, as he finishes up his letter to him, he mentions some of the other soldiers who have shared in the campaign—as it were, he encloses a few snapshots which Timothy will love to see. We, too, will perhaps be interested to take a look at them. Here's the first; but—what is this written on the back?

A Base Deserter

"*Demas has forsaken me, having loved this present world, and has departed for Thessalonica.*" That had possibly been coming on for a long while. In Philemon 24, Paul had said, "Demas . . . my fellow laborer"—as if he had shared as fully as any of the others in the work; but in Colossians 4:14 he wrote, ". . . and Demas"— with no added encomium or remark of any kind, as if, according to Dr. James Spence, "he was beginning to suspect him, to mark worldliness creeping over his spirit." Ah yes, (*a*) *A worldly spirit*— what damage that has done to Christians and to the Church. I wonder what form it took with Demas? I wonder if John Bunyan's *Pilgrim's Progress* is right in holding that it was money? You remember the incident of the silver mine. Of course, this spirit manifests itself in many ways. Sometimes it is, as Bunyan suggests, (1) Possessions—a lust to get, a policy of grab. Many an earnest believer, beginning to get rich, has been spiritually ruined in this way. Money in itself is not wrong—many wealthy people have been outstandingly godly; but money ill-gotten is "dishonest gain" (Titus 1:11), and money loved is "a root of all kinds of evil" (1 Timothy 6:10). It is the believer's wisdom to be on his guard about this. (2) Pleasure—how reasonable a thing, to be sure; but how ruinous it can become. It makes for good health, both physical and spiritual, to allow room for relaxation and enjoyment; one of the rare aids to poise and balance is a capacity for fun. Yet, how completely it can run away with us if we are not careful. We may, I think, legitimately enjoy our pleasures provided they are of the right kind, at the right time, and in the right proportion. (3) Popularity—it is nice to be popular; it may, indeed, be a help in our Christian service if we are popular; but what a snare! Many a Christian has done wrong things, has left undone right things, because of the fear of losing a too-much-prized popularity. After all, it is not what "they" will think, but what He will. (4) Pride—a thing peculiarly ugly in a believer, but which a worldly spirit will so readily engender. (5) Present life—the habit of looking at things from the viewpoint of the present. It is really surprising how many Christians have acquired this "squint." You can understand it in the worldling; but it is dreadfully out of place in a believer. It was because he restricted his vision to what was "under the sun" that the "Preacher" of Ecclesiastes found himself in such perplexity.

You will observe that this worldly spirit in Demas was accompanied by (*b*) *A cowardly spirit*—He "departed"! The Greek word is an entirely different one from that which we studied in verse 6 last time. There was nothing splendid, ennobling, enriching, about this man's going. (1) Why did he go? Well, the persecution of

Christians was in the air; to have abode with Paul, to have been known as one of them, was to court trouble; better go while the going was good. So he "departed" from Rome. (2) Where did he go? To Thessalonica, where there was a body of believers. That, to my mind, indicates that Demas had no intention of ceasing to be a Christian: all he proposed to himself was that he should no longer be an out-and-out Christian. Yet, did he but know it, he was letting himself in for a very uncomfortable time by going there of all places; for at Thessalonica the Christians were very keen; and, besides, they were great friends of Paul's. We have only to read between the lines of 1 and 2 Thessalonians to discover both those facts. But, then, a half-hearted Christian always will be uncomfortable wherever he is. Like a man with a headache—who doesn't want to lose his head, but it hurts him to keep it; so this Christian doesn't want to lose his religion, but it hurts him to keep it. Thus wrote Hannah W. Smith in *The Christian's Secret of a Happy Life*. Dr. Alexander Maclaren's summing up of Demas is "He was a religious man who had not religion enough to resist the constant attractions and seductions of the present." I will only add that, through the hole made in his consecration, his courage also leaked away.

But enough. Let's look at another "snap": what does it say? Oh yes—

One of the Rank and File

"*Crescens for Galatia.*" Never heard of him! No; he was only a private, only an ordinary soldier; but here he is, mentioned in dispatches. How much God's cause is advanced by ordinary, unknown people. I was so struck the other day in reading Hebrews 11 to notice how, after the recital of those great and ever-glorious names, there follows "And others" (verse 35), "Still others" (verse 36)—just anonymous heroes of the faith. Or, think of the prestige and powers of that distinguished company in 1 Corinthians 12:28: "God has appointed these in the church: first apostles, second prophets, third teachers, after that miracles, then gifts of healings . . . administrations, varieties of tongues." An important group: but what have ordinary folk to do with such? There seems little room for us among them. But wait: that vacant place we have left in the list is occupied in the text by "helps." Why, the rank and file can be that! Have you ever heard of Hanani? No? You have heard of Nehemiah, then? Yes; but you wouldn't have if it had not been for Hanani. It was he who lit the flame in the famous man's heart: Nehemiah was a torch, a name for God, but Hanani was the match that lit the torch. Who was Edward Kimball? You don't know? Of course not: he was only a shoemaker and a humble Sunday school teacher. He, too, was a match; and his torch was D. L. Moody! Maria Millis, of whom I am sure you have never heard, was another. She was an old-fashioned family nurse. She loved God; and she loved the little boy, Ashley, in her charge. In his heart she planted the seed and tended it. You have not heard of her, but you have heard of him—Lord Shaftesbury! How many such have advanced the cause. Crescens was that sort, one of the rank and file.

Now, another "snap": this is inscribed—

A Distinguished Officer

"*Titus for Dalmatia.*" This was no ordinary man. (*a*) *He was a leader.* We badly need such: those who, in the church, or in the home, or in the office, or in the workshop, or in any group will set the tone, give a lead, in a nice, clean, healthy, strong, wise, godly direction. No need, here, to be forever "preaching": just a touch, a word, a look, an attitude. Let us not leave leadership to the devil and his agents. Titus had an exalted sphere for his leadership, he was Bishop of Crete; we may exercise ours in humbler realms—but let us, wherever we be, take pains that we lead life in right, and in Christian, channels.

The secret of Titus' successful leadership was (*b*) *He was led.* Joshua became Moses' successor because he had been such a success as "Moses' assistant" (Joshua 1:1); he led so well, because he had learned to follow. Mark how Titus was led and you will not be surprised that he was a leader. (1) First, he was led *to* Christ. Paul did that for him (Titus 1:4) as he did for Timothy (1 Timothy 1:2). (2) Then, he was led *for* Christ. The apostle followed up the work of grace in his heart, nurturing him for the Master and leading him on in His service. The Epistle to Titus is part of the wonderful preparation he gave him for his task. (3) And so, he was led *by* Christ into all kinds of service, and into rich depths of spiritual experience. It was with Titus, as it would be for any, that because he followed so closely he led so well.

It is a pity we have to hurry over these pictures—that there is so little space to enlarge on them; but, after all, they are only snapshots. Well, pick up another: what's this that it says?—

The M.O.

"*Only Luke is with me.*" Do you remember (*a*) *When he first joined the Army*? It seems to have been at Troas, where Dr. Luke had a general practice. If we may try to reconstruct the scene: One day he was called out to see a patient, a visitor to the town who had been taken ill. It was a man named Paul. When the doctor got to the house where Paul had taken lodgings, he found the man feverish and shaking and pretty bad. He quickly diagnosed malaria; and we can well imagine what this meant to this restless, tireless man. It would trouble him all his life; for this was (I think, following Sir William Ramsay, as I do) the "thorn in the flesh" from which he was never freed (2 Corinthians 12:7–9). However, as always happens to the true Christian's circumstances (Romans 8:28), the Lord overruled this attack for his good: it brought Dr. Luke to Paul, and Paul brought Dr. Luke to Christ. Thus the good doctor enlisted in the army of the Lord and was a member of the expeditionary force that embarked upon the Macedonian Campaign. Note the "we" of Acts 16:10.

See (*b*) *What he contributed to the campaign*—preeminently, of course, his medical gifts, for he was the Medical Officer of the regiment and the first medical missionary; then, too, there were his literary gifts, for he had a vivid and often intensely beautiful style of writing which proved of great service to the cause. Who can measure the extent of the usefulness of his Gospel and of his Acts? And we should not forget his personal gifts, the charm of manner, the attractiveness of personality that he very evidently possessed. All he had, and all he was, was gladly thrown into the cause. May we stay a moment to ask ourselves whether such complete abandonment to God marks *our* Christian life?

Note (*c*) *What he meant to the C.O.* First, in fidelity. From Troas to Philippi, where he was stationed for a while to nurture the young believers; afterwards, back to Jerusalem, up to Caesarea, on the sea during the terrible storm and shipwreck, across to Rome during the first imprisonment, and now under the awful conditions of the second imprisonment—Luke scarcely left his side; and, for the moment, he is the "only" companion he has. What a help it must have been for him to have a doctor on the mission party all those years. Then, in affection, how much he would mean. Unless I am greatly mistaken, Paul set great store by the loving-kindness of his friends. Over and over again you see, in his letters, expressions of his gratitude for their help and gifts. And when in Colossians 4:14 you read "Luke the beloved physician," you can detect the deep mutual affection that existed between these two.

But, alas, we have spent as much time as we dare over this attractive man. Let us pick up another snapshot: it is inscribed—

A Credit to the Regiment

"*Get Mark and bring him with you, for he is useful to me for ministry.*" But surely I have seen this young man somewhere before? I seem to remember something rather shady about him. Yes, you are quite right: there was (*a*) *His past failure.* There is no burking it, he had been a disgrace to the regiment. Do you recall how enthusiastically he had begun? Soon after his conversion, which happened through Peter, as 1 Peter 5:13 seems to suggest, he was introduced to Paul by his uncle Barnabas, and thenceforth he threw all the virility of his ardent young manhood into the cause, joining, as Acts 13:5 shows, the first missionary party. They had a grand time in Cyprus—the equable climate, the Christian adventure, and the spiritual triumphs combined with the daily companionship of the two great men to make it for Mark an unforgettable experience. And then, alas, the tragedy happened. They crossed over to Pamphylia, which the young enthusiast quickly discovered to be a fever-laden area. I suspect that this was where Paul picked up his malaria germ. Mark was too scared to go on; and, begging to be excused the remainder of the tour, he returned home to his mother at Jerusalem.

There is no need here to recall the sad consequences of this defection; for we must hurry on to (*b*) *His present condition.* By the grace of God, and perhaps through the tender handling of Barnabas, he climbed out of the morass and has actually become a credit to the regiment—"he is useful to me." Paul had already used that word when, in 2:21, he spoke of the man who was "useful for the Master"—useful to the Master. And now Paul applied it to Mark: useful to His servant, useful all round. That is a quality which we might all covet, to be ever ready to help both Him and His. It is very delightful to observe the change that has come over the relationship between these two men. Paul had, very firmly, and, as I think, very rightly, refused the employment of the younger man; but now he is reinstated. A work of grace had been going on—possibly through Barnabas' behavior, for I think that he also was right. Paul now badly wants the very man that once he wouldn't have.

Another thing, as I look at his snapshot, that I am reminded of is (*c*) *His prospective honor.* We never can tell what God has in mind for the returning backslider. For Mark it was something unspeakably honorable: God had chosen him to be the writer of the Gospel according to Mark. If any of my readers has, like Mark, wandered from God and deserted His service, will he, also like Mark, come back? You will not be commissioned to write a Gospel, but you will be expected to live one—

> *"You are writing a Gospel, a chapter each day,*
> *By all that you do, and all that you say.*
> *Men read what you write, whether faithless, or true,*
> *Say, what is the gospel according to you?"*

"This honor have all His saints," if I may dare to adopt the words of Psalm 149:9, spoken in a very different connection.

So, ere we put the little snapshot down, let us take notice of one further point, (*d*) *His perennial lesson.* It is, that there is always a way back home for the backslider. Think of Jonah, renegade and runaway. He was offered the inestimable privilege of going to a heathen people to proclaim the message of repentance unto salvation; but his insensate prejudice forbade him, and he ran away from God! But, of course, when a man runs away from God, then God runs after him. In miraculous ways, God, at great pains, turned him back, and, greatest miracle of all, He offered him again the same task: "The word of the Lord came to Jonah the second time" (Jonah 3:1). Or, again, think of Peter. How earnest he was in the Master's service. He meant every word he said; yet, at the testing time, he failed terribly and "went out and wept bitterly" (Luke 22:62). Was that the end? "I will heal their backsliding" is God's promise, through Hosea 14:4, to every truly repentant soul. He did that for Peter, and for Jonah, and for Mark; He will still do it for any of His children who stray from

Him, however deep they have sunk.

> *"Have you sinn'd as none else in the world have before?*
> *Are you blacker than other creatures in guilt?*
> *Oh, fear not, and doubt not! the mother who bore you*
> *Loves you less than the Savior whose blood you have spilt.*

> *"Come, come to His feet, and lay open your story*
> *Of suffering and sorrow, of guilt and of shame;*
> *For the pardon of sin is the crown of His glory,*
> *And the joy of our Lord to be true to His name."*

Faber's intensely moving lines are blessedly true, as a myriad could testify. Just one more snapshot—

The Colonel's Batman

"*Tychicus I have sent to Ephesus.*" There is a fuller portrait of this man to be seen in the group photograph in Colossians 4:7–14, where Paul outlines his character as (*a*) "*A beloved brother*"; —brother, because master and servant each were alike children in God's family, through "common faith" (Titus 1:4) in Christ; beloved, because he had learned his true worth and esteemed him highly. And (*b*) "*A fellow servant*"—if Tychicus was Paul's servant, both of them were the Lord's servants, "bondslaves of Jesus Christ." But dwell just now on the middle point, (*c*) "*A faithful minister*"— the word used seems to signify his personal servant, almost his valet; in military language, his batman. Paul had long since discovered how utterly trustworthy he was and sent him on many a delicate mission. For example, when he had written the Epistle to the Colossians, this was the man to whom he entrusted its safe delivery. (Incidentally, he arranged that Onesimus, bearing the letter to Philemon, should travel with Tychicus so that if Onesimus "funked" it at the last moment, he might prevent his running away again.) And now he has sent him "to Ephesus." That was where Timothy's headquarters were, and Paul wanted Timothy to come to him. I surmise that Tychicus went to relieve Timothy and, in some degree, to hold the fort till he returned. But, in that case, what was Paul to do in Tychicus' absence for the more personal service that he needed? I suggest that that was why Timothy was asked to pick up Mark on his way to Rome and bring him along with him—"for ministry": it is the same word, in the Greek, as is applied in Colossians 4:7 to Tychicus. May the Master, whose "bondservants" we are, find us as "faithful" in every duty and on every day as those two were to Paul.

And now, as we close, let us drop all this military metaphor and go back to those poignant and pathetic words with which the portion opened: "Be diligent to come to me quickly." They are the urgent message of a dying father who hasn't long now to live, and who so greatly longs to have one last look, and touch, of a beloved son. "Do your very best to come to me as quickly as ever you can"—anyhow "before winter," he adds in verse 21. The mantle of that intimate relationship was spread over the opening passages of the epistle, and at its close we find it extended again. I don't think we have gone far wrong in the title we have given these studies.

ON REMAND

2 Timothy 4:13–18

13. Bring the cloak that I left with Carpus at Troas when you come—and the books, especially the parchments.
14. Alexander the coppersmith did me much harm. May the Lord repay him according to his works.
15. You also must beware of him, for he has greatly resisted our words.
16. At my first defense no one stood with me, but all forsook me. May it not be charged against them.
17. But the Lord stood with me and strengthened me, so that the message might be preached fully through me, and that all the Gentiles might hear. And I was delivered out of the mouth of the lion.
18. And the Lord will deliver me from every evil work and preserve me for His heavenly kingdom. To Him be glory forever and ever. Amen!

17

ON REMAND

2 Timothy 4:13–18

LET me remind you that, after his release from his first Roman imprisonment, Paul enjoyed three or four years of freedom to pursue again his peripatetic ministry in the gospel, after which he was rearrested—perhaps at Troas—and it is from out of this second imprisonment that 2 Timothy comes.

There seems to be some kind of a break after verse 8 of our present chapter, and verse 9 bears a disjointed appearance. Dr. Eugene Stock, in his *Plain Talks on the Pastoral Epistles* (p. 306), gives reason for his inclining to the view that, at the conclusion of his writing verse 8, Paul was taken off to his trial in the Emperor's Court. There he had unexpectedly secured an adjournment and was returned to his prison on remand. He had imagined that he was to be immediately sent to his death, and the verses he had just finished have all the air of a final farewell; but now a further breathing space is afforded him and, with the customary postponements of the then legal procedure—who knows how long that may be—there may yet be time for him to get one last loving visit from dear Timothy. So, once again, he turns to complete his letter, speaking after a different fashion from what he had at first intended. He urges Timothy, as we saw last lecture, to come to him as quickly as possible, and meanwhile tells him something of what had happened in court. We are to think, then, of our present passage as dictated while on remand, and it will remind us of—

The Rigor of His Cell

How very different his present conditions are from those of his former detention can be estimated by reading Acts 28:30–31. That had been a lenient imprisonment; but now, in the Mamertine Prison, he is in the underground dungeon—damp and dark, and dismal and dirty, and dreadfully cold. So he asks that Timothy will bring him some things that would alleviate his distress, things that he had hurriedly left behind when, perhaps, he had been suddenly arrested at Troas and given no time even to collect a bit of luggage. I cannot otherwise account for Paul leaving "the parchments" behind, as we shall see presently. These things were in the care of Carpus—a gentleman about whom we know practically nothing. Evidently he was a friend of Paul's, and that's good enough: anyone who was a friend of his is one whom I should be proud to know. I love his name; it means Fruit: one of the many "fruits" of Paul's ministry, I suppose. By the way, have you, my reader, any fruits of your service for God? So, in the house of this friend and fruit of his were these things that Paul longed to have. Dean Farrar, in his great book on St. Paul, calls attention to the interesting similarity in the life of William Tyndale, who from his prison at Vilvorden in 1535 asked for some warmer clothing and above all for his Hebrew Bible and grammar and dictionary. Well, our apostle asks for—

(*a*) *Something to warm his body*—"the cloak." It was perishing cold in that cell, especially with winter approaching, as verse 21 reminds us. The word means a circular garment, sleeveless with a hole in the middle for slipping it over the head, like a bicycle cape. It would be made of the black goat's hair that was so familiar. I wonder where the apostle bought it? Or—perhaps he made it himself? Remember that tents were made of this same material; and Paul was a tentmaker. Anyhow, it had been a great comfort to him on his travels, and if only he could get it now, it would wonderfully palliate the rigor of his cell. Do you wonder that the Bible should find room for the mention of such an ordinary everyday thing as the need of a cloak? Bishop Moule would answer you that "the God of Scripture has room in His heart for every detail of human life." All the little things of your life are an interest to Him; all the little needs you have are a concern to Him—so don't hesitate to bring them to Him in your prayers. It became the fashion, in certain high ecclesiastical circles, to say that this cloak was a eucharistic vestment like a chasuble, and that Paul needed it for ritualistic purposes! An "astounding suggestion," says Dr. Plummer; and Bishop Bernard, "a perverse idea." Next, Paul wanted—

(b) *Something to occupy his mind*—"the books." They would be papyrus rolls. I wonder what were the subjects, and who the authors? It would be fascinating to know what books he had thus collected and so greatly valued. Professor David Smith says they were "probably memoranda of his own." I do not know what right he has to say "probably"; perhaps we may be allowed to soften it and say "possibly." Doubtless the apostle kept records of things, and people, and sayings, and events, and it would be a great refreshment to him to go over these reminiscences. Perhaps the idea of getting the books was to be able to read through them with Dr. Luke, and to bequeath them to him on his death. In that case, they would be of inestimable value to the good doctor and author when he was compiling his book of Acts of the Apostles. We know from Luke 1:1–4 that, speaking of the human side of the matter, it was by using the work of other writers, etc., that he constructed his own histories. Then Paul asked for—

(c) *Something to feed his soul*—"the parchments." I take it, they would be parts of the Scriptures, and that was why he "especially" wanted them. But are you not surprised that a man like

Paul should leave his Bible behind like that? That is what inclines me to accept the idea that he was arrested at Troas—perhaps somewhere on the street, and given no permission even to call at his lodgings to collect his belongings. Bundled off in that fashion, he had perforce to leave behind his warm overcoat, his little library of books, and, what mattered "especially," his Bible. I can imagine how insistently he would impress upon us the importance of always having our Bible near at hand and, what is more important still, of always living our lives near to our Bible! And now, as he continues to dictate his letter, there rises up before his mind—

The Figure of His Adversary

"Alexander the coppersmith"—or, as it should be, just "the smith," whether copper or other. That must put out of court the old churchwarden's joke on counting the collection with a preponderance of the cheapest coins: "Alexander the coppersmith has done us much evil." It was a feeble joke, and called for a quick death; but, but—in any case—why make jokes out of Bible things? Surely there are plenty of other places to get them from, without desecrating holy ground. I do most seriously protest that we Christians should refrain ourselves from any sort of flippant treatment of God's Book. And, having got that off my mind, let me invite you to consider the figure of this sinister personality who proved to be Paul's antagonist-in-chief at this time.

First notice (*a*) *His position in the matter*—"did me much harm." On this, Mr. Shaw Caldecott, in his *Synthetic Studies in Scripture*, says, "It has been left to a learned Indian judge to discover that, in the words translated '. . . did me much evil' [A.V.], we have an old legal formula of Roman times, the modern equivalent of which is, '. . . laid the information against me.'" It was on the sworn information of this man that the case proceeded. I find that Conybeare and Howson render the phrase,

". . . charged me with much evil": the same thing as His Honor the judge said. What a dreadful reputation to have on the page of history—to have been the initiating cause of the arrest, and trial, and martyrdom of the grand apostle. May it be ours, on the contrary, to be the initiating cause of much blessing and many lives saved.

The next point to be considered about "Alexander Smith" is (*b*) *His peril for believers*—"you also must beware of him, for he has greatly resisted our words." If you turn to 1 Timothy 1:20, you will read of "Hymenaeus and Alexander, whom I delivered to Satan that they may learn not to blaspheme." We have no evidence either way, but I have a very distinct suspicion that this is the same Alexander. It was, of course, a quite common name, and there may have been two persons; but it would so fit into things if they were the same. At the time of that earlier passage, he has been falling into such grave sin that Paul has felt compelled to deliver his body into Satan's hands that his soul may be saved. Hymenaeus, you remember, is mentioned in our 2:17; and now, I think, it is Alexander his companion in iniquity. He has had to wait a year or so for his revenge; and, at the time of this (4:14), his chance has come to get his own back for evil. Circumstances have arisen which the tortuous and iniquitous mind of Alexander can twist into a charge against the apostle, and so an "information" is laid with the law authorities. Moreover, if our conjecture be right, this man had been one of the Christian company; he would know what was done, what was said, what was thought; he could as easily trap the other Christians as he had trapped Paul—therefore "you also must beware of him." Such a rebellious sheep would always be a danger; but he would be all the more dangerous because he was at one time numbered among the flock. None is so fierce an enemy as an erstwhile friend.

Look, however, at (*c*) *His punishment by God*—"may the Lord repay him according to his works." Does that sound vindictive? Are you surprised that such a man as Paul would talk like that? Well, it all depends upon whether he is thinking of Alexander's damage as being done to himself or to the cause. The Master Himself observed that distinction. When did He ever reproach men for their doing harm to Himself personally? When, in our present passage, Paul speaks of those who have hurt him, his tone is very different, as we shall see presently in verse 16. It is the hurt he has done to the cause which calls forth this prayer from the apostle's outraged soul. Note Paul's reference to "*our* words," as if he were speaking and thinking collectively, not "*my* words," as if he were considering the matter individually and personally. But if I do not in this carry you with me, let me invite your attention to the fact that, following the weight of manuscript authority, the Revised Version has here, "the Lord *will* render to him"—not a prayer for God to do it, but a statement that He will do it! Psalm 62:12 had said, "You render to each one according to his work." So this is the man who started all the trouble. Consider, in the last place—

The Vigor of His Defense

"At my first defense," says Paul in verse 16—that is, his first answer to the charge brought against him. His second answer will be made after his remand, when the case comes up for resumed hearing. The astonishing fact was that (*a*) *No one would undertake his defense.* (1) Professional pleaders refused the case— "no one stood with me"; the verb is used in a technical, legal sense, as of what we would call defending counsel. I suppose they were afraid of getting mixed up in such a charge and being tarred with the same brush; for I have no doubt that, as the Jewish leaders did in all these cases against the Christians, they proffered here an accusation of sedition and treason. Why, they even did that in the case of our Lord: recall the words in Luke 23:2, "We found this fellow perverting the nation, and forbidding to pay taxes to Caesar, saying that He Himself is . . . a king." It was, of course, a trumped-up charge; but the Roman authorities would never have listened to the real trouble, the religious question. The same thing happened with Paul at Thessalonica in Acts 17:7, "these all are acting contrary to the decrees of Caesar, saying there is another king—Jesus." I should think that once again the apostle was the victim of this fraudulent behavior, and that is why no lawyer could be found to help him. Moreover, it seems to me that even (2) Witnesses absented themselves—"all forsook me," all those, that is, that should have been there to testify in his favor. Their evidence might have been of enormous assistance, but they let him down—for the same reason, I presume, that had weighed with the lawyers. The accused man felt their defection very keenly; of course he did. But, as bearing out what we said earlier, will you note his reaction—"May it not be charged against them." No shadow of vengefulness is here, but sweet prayerfulness. But, where have I heard like words before? Where has Paul heard like words before? Ah yes—it was more than thirty years ago that, as a young leader, he had presided at a Christian's execution, and, as the cruel stones crushed the life out of the sufferer, the grand martyr, Stephen, had prayed, "Lord, do not charge them with this sin" (Acts 7:60). That scene was one of the smarting stabs that (Acts 9:5) pricked his conscience; and those words had remained in his memory ever since, and only now, after thirty long years and faced with his own martyrdom, could he empathize fully with Stephen by praying the same prayer for those who despitefully used him and persecuted him. They both caught that lovely spirit from the Savior—even as we get all of good from Him—when He asked, "Father, forgive them, for they do not know what they do" (Luke 23:34).

So here Paul is in the old Roman court, left all alone; and (*b*) *He conducted his own defense.* Never an easy thing to do; sometimes a dangerous thing to do; but, in this instance, there was no help for it. How typical it was of Paul that in this (1) He saw an opportunity—"That the message might be preached fully through me"; instead of the bits and extracts, and rumors, of what he had taught that may have reached them, he could now give them a full account of his message. The Acts of the Apostles shows us how he took the opportunity that his various trials afforded him of making his message fully known, telling of Jesus of Nazareth as the Lord of glory come down to earth, who went about doing good, whom they crucified, but God raised Him, and all who believe on Him shall receive remission of sins and be filled with the Holy Spirit. Paul's defense would be the strangest that ever they had heard: there was practically nothing about himself, it was all about his Lord. "And that all the Gentiles might hear," that is, all the Gentiles there in that court. There was Nero, or if he was absent (as some think he was at this time away on Imperial business in Greece) there was Burrus, the Prefect of the city of Rome who acted for the Emperor in his absence. Then there were all the court officials, and besides them the general public who would crowd the place upon such an occasion. What a chance, thinks Paul, that all these shall have a full explanation of the saving message! Don't you think it would be well if, every day of our lives, we were very definitely, and very earnestly, to ask God to help us to see, and to seize, opportunities? Biography is one of my hobbies; and out of a fairly wide acquaintance with the lives of successful servants of God and ardent soul-winners, I should say that, in every case, a great part of their secret was this alertness to sudden opportunity. What now was the upshot of Paul's action? (2) He secured a remand—"I was delivered out of the mouth of the lion." That old lion who, according to 1 Peter 5:8, "walks about . . . seeking whom he may devour," was for the moment robbed of his prey. Dr. Plummer says that "the deliverance does not mean release from prison following upon acquittal, but temporary rescue from imminent danger."

Paul would not, however, have us forget that (*c*) *The Lord was his defense*—"But the Lord stood with me and strengthened me." His unfailing presence, and His upholding power, were at Paul's disposal though all else fail. He, and we, can always rely on that, however lonely and deserted we may feel. One is reminded of what the Master said in John 16:32 about Himself, "you . . . will leave Me alone. And yet I am not alone, because the Father is with Me." Alone; and yet not alone! And, thank God, what was His comfort is our comfort too, and was Paul's. The teacher in a Sunday school class was explaining to her scholars the words "I will never leave you," in Hebrews 13:5, when one of the boys, a sparkling little Irishman, suddenly interrupted, "I see, teacher, I see what it means. What it means is, that when there's only one of us, there's always two of us!" Very Irish? Yes; but very true, and very precious. Have you ever had to go and do some difficult piece of work, to bear some definite witness, when you were all alone and feeling it? There was only one of you. No; two! Paul was seemingly all alone in that court, but he wasn't really alone: he was one, the mighty One was the other. And, as someone once said, "One with God is a majority."

That was, of course, the real reason why he secured a remand; and, with the assurance of faith, he adds, "And the Lord will deliver me from every evil work," the corollary of which is that anything we are not delivered from is not, in true perspective, evil. The very same thing that he was spared on remand happened to him at his retrial, so that by then it had assumed something of good, according to his own testimony in Romans 8:28. He knows that his Lord will "preserve" him until the good time comes for his translation to "His heavenly kingdom." To that Lord he would give "glory"; and to His will he would say "Amen." The scholars have remarked on the similarity of this verse to the words of the Lord's Prayer; and, inasmuch as the Gospels had not by this time been written, they draw the conclusion that the Prayer had been widely taught orally and was familiar to those early believers—and was known in the longer version that Matthew subsequently gave us, with the doxology (6:13). Be that as it may, we would close by inviting you to join in Paul's "Amen" to that "sweet beloved will," that "wonderful grand will," that "will that willest good alone"—as Tersteegen's hymn describes it. How Paul would reecho the line as he goes back on remand and as he subsequently returns to trial again: "Upon God's will I lay me down."

JUST A LAST FEW LINES

2 Timothy 4:19–22

19. Greet Prisca and Aquila, and the household of Onesiphorus.
20. Erastus stayed in Corinth, but Trophimus I have left in Miletus sick.
21. Do your utmost to come before winter. Eubulus greets you, as well as Pudens, Linus, Claudia, and all the brethren.
22. The Lord Jesus Christ be with your spirit. Grace be with you. Amen.

18

JUST A LAST FEW LINES

2 Timothy 4:19–22

IT was Paul's custom to dictate his letters to someone who would act as his amanuensis. We do not know whether they were taken down in shorthand. That was a possibility, because this useful accomplishment was not invented by Isaac Pitman in 1837; many systems had existed long before Sir Isaac's day, and indeed, it was practiced extensively by the Romans away back in Cicero's time, 106–43 B.C., many of whose speeches were "taken down." For all we know, then, Dr. Luke, who presumably took down this letter, may have added stenography to his many other gifts. What we are sure of is that Paul always added a few closing lines in his own hand, as 2 Thessalonians 3:17 tells us—"The salutation of Paul with my own hand, which is a sign in every epistle; so I write." There is, if my understanding of it is correct, a rather emotional ending to his Colossian letter, which he concludes by writing, "This salutation by my own hand—Paul. Remember my chains . . ." (4:18). Why does he add that last bit? Well, as we know, he was, during the imprisonment, chained at the wrist to a Roman soldier; and whatever his normal handwriting was like, it could not have been improved by that circumstance. I suggest that, when he saw what a bad fist he had made of it, he adds those words about his chains by way of explanation and extenuation. Our present passage, following that first "Amen," would appear to be his personally written addition to this particular letter and was presumably the last thing he ever did write. Let us note three things—

First—Personalities

He has already mentioned fifteen people in the course of his dictation, and now he writes of eight others; the ninth name here occurs earlier. (*a*) *Some are in Ephesus, where Timothy is*—and the apostle bids him give them his kind remembrance, his affectionate greetings. (1) Prisca and Aquila. Six times this splendid couple are referred to in the New Testament, and in four of the instances the lady, as here, is put first. Is the suggestion fanciful that this possibly indicates that she was the leading spirit in the partnership, so far as spiritual things were concerned? It seems probable that Paul first made their acquaintance in the way of business. When he first arrived with the gospel at Corinth, he determined to support himself by his tentmaking. Every Jewish boy, however genteel the family, was taught some trade; and Paul had often to be thankful for his proficiency in this craft. As it happened, there were two Jewish refugees at Corinth at the time. They had come from Rome, whence all Jews had been expelled by the Emperor Claudius about A.D. 53. "The emperors more than once expelled them from the city, but they always returned," comments the late Professor H. M. Gwatkin, in his grand *Early Church History* (Vol. 1, p. 40). As a matter of fact, these two are back in Rome in Romans 16:3. Their trade was tentmaking, and they had "set up shop" at Corinth, and when Paul came across their sign, he secured, as Acts 18:1–3 recounts, both work and lodging with them, thus supporting himself, and giving himself in his spare time, and on the sabbaths, to the preaching of the gospel. It was not long until, as had previously happened with his doctor, he led his landlady and landlord to Christ. I wonder if part of the influence he exerted on them was due to the efficient way in which he did his work? It is recorded of Joseph, in Genesis 39:3, that "his master saw that the Lord was with him"—a something about the way he did his work? And perhaps Paul's employers were impressed with the fidelity and dexterity with which he set about his daily tasks, and were all the more readily disposed to listen when he spoke to them of his Master. Let all those take special note of this point who, being Christians, are in domestic service, or at a workshop bench, or on an office stool, or at a school desk. "His master saw"—and of course, his Master saw! Anyhow, the two are converted; and how quickly they grow, for by Acts 18:26, having passed on to Ephesus, they were able to take the greatly gifted Apollos and to "explain to him the way of God more accurately." Their loyalty and courage are next to be observed, for Romans 16:4 says they "risked their own necks for my life"—in some ugly situation they had risked their necks to save the apostle. Unlike those nobles of Nehemiah 3:5, who "did not put their shoulders [literally, *necks*] to the work of their Lord," these two were "up to their necks" in it. Finally, in 1 Corinthians 16:19, we find them lending the accommodation of their home for the gathering of the believers for worship: "the church that is in their house." A fine pair of devoted Christians: no wonder Paul sends them, through Timothy, his affectionate greetings.

(2) The household of Onesiphorus is also greeted. We dealt with them at 1:16. Onesiphorus himself, as not being included in the good wishes, was obviously absent, either because he had died or, as I think, was away on some journey. "He often refreshed me," says the apostle—recalling wistfully the delightful hospitality he had enjoyed in that home. Led by the Spirit, Paul had joined with Peter (Romans 12:13; 1 Timothy 3:2; Titus 1:8; 1 Peter 4:9) in pressing upon believers the duty and virtue of Christian hospitality—all the more needful, perhaps, in those early days when believers were few and scattered; but still greatly fruitful in these days.

Continuing our study of these recorded personalities, we see (*b*) *Some are in Rome, where Paul is.* Each of them "greets" Timothy—there is Eubulus, Pudens, Linus, and Claudia. Various flimsy identifications of these people have been attempted, but they may quite safely be ignored, with one exception. Says Dr. Handley Moule, "More solid, for early tradition favors it, and there lies no difficulty in the way, is the belief that the Linus here named is the first Christian pastor to be entrusted with the bishopric of Rome in the early and holy simplicity of that great office." Dr. Alfred Plummer may also usefully be quoted: "We may safely conclude that the Linus who here sends greeting is identical with the Linus who, according to very early testimony preserved by Irenaeus, was first among the earliest bishops of the church of Rome. Irenaeus himself expressly identifies the [two]." "And all the brethren," proceeds our passage—all the church in that city, called "brethren" because members of the same family. (1) What a large family we are—"the blessed company of all faithful [believing] people," as the Church of England Prayer Book describes them, embracing all believers, the first, the last, and the rest. At any given time, or spot, seen to be a "little flock," but in the eternal aggregate, a "great multitude" (Luke 12:32; Revelation 7:9). (2) What a loving family we should be—the bickering, quarreling, criticizing, that disgrace some earthly families should never disfigure the family of God. And having written that, I hang my head with shame, and pass sadly on to (3) What a loyal family we should be—loyal to one another; but, above all, loyal to the Head of the Family.

But now (*c*) *Some are elsewhere.* (1) At Corinth—was Erastus. He is, I expect, the same man as is mentioned in Acts 19:22, who had accompanied Timothy on a certain mission to Macedonia. They would have got to know each other very well on that trip; and Timothy would be glad to have news of him. So he "stayed in Corinth," did he? Well, that was where he belonged; indeed, he was a person of some considerable position there, being, as Romans 16:23 tells us, "the treasurer of the city." What a splendid thing for any municipality when there are avowed Christians in its important posts. I am presuming again, you see, that the same name here means the same person. You and I, my reader, have some position in the municipality, whether high or humble, whether an employee or a citizen: may we seek to influence the civic life of our town in any way, big or small, that comes to our hand as avowed Christians, pulling our weight on behalf of everything that is clean, and true, and beautiful for the community, acting "on the side of the angels," as Benjamin Disraeli would say, "for you serve the Lord Christ," as Paul would say (Colossians 3:24). Then (2) At Miletus—was Trophimus. He, too, taking the references to denote the same person, is mentioned in two other places. In Acts 20:4 his name is included in the list of helpers in one of Paul's mission parties; and in Acts 21:29 he is the innocent cause of Paul's being mobbed at Jerusalem; but it is the account of him here in our present passage that I want particularly to look at, and I shall do so under our following heading—

Next—Humanities

Paul was so remarkable a character that we are sometimes in danger of forgetting that he was only human after all. This latter quality peeps out here, in (*a*) *His human limitations*—"Trophimus I have left in Miletus sick." Yet it would seem that he would have been so helpful to the apostle's work if only he had been made well enough to go on, instead of having to be left behind; and Paul had remarkable healing powers entrusted to him as we learn from Acts 19:11–12: "God worked unusual miracles by the hands of Paul, so that even handkerchiefs or aprons were brought from his body to the sick, and the diseases left them. . . ." Yes, but you see if we take the whole Scripture testimony, and eschew the one-text method, we are, I believe, driven to the conclusion that bodily healing is not always the will of God. Why, even Paul himself was handicapped by obstinate ill-health, a "thorn in the flesh," which I personally follow Sir William Ramsay in thinking was malaria. How much more, and how much better service he would be able to render to the cause, if he could get rid of this persistent infirmity. So he prayed God, for His own glory, to heal him; three times he very specially prayed about it, with what result we know from 2 Corinthians 12:8–10—God did not heal him; but what was harder, gave him "grace" to triumph over it. And Timothy, too: what a pity, and what a hindrance, that he should remain something of an invalid, with his frequent attacks of gastric trouble; whereas, with a robust constitution, he could wage so intrepid a fight. Why, then, did Paul not heal him? Why was it that the best he could do was to prescribe a regular vinous dosage for his "frequent infirmities" (1 Timothy 5:23)? Paul had his gifts, his powers, but he was only human and his great possibilities were subject to the limitation of God's perfect will and purpose.

We observe here also (*b*) *His human longings*—"Do your utmost to come before winter." Under the restrictions of the primitive navigation of those days, there was no sailing in the winter; and if Timothy did not get away before then, it would necessitate a long dreary postponement of his visit, and in all probability it would then come too late. And this very human father did so badly want to see his son. In verse 9 he had already dictated, "Be diligent to come to me quickly," but now, in his own handwriting, he pens it, "Do your utmost to come before winter." The Master would not upbraid him for this humanity: He, too, was so truly human that he leaned in the Garden on the prayerful sympathy of His three intimate friends, as we saw in an earlier lecture.

The fact is, the new birth does not deprive us of our humanities. A great treasure has become ours; but, as 2 Corinthians 4:7

tells us, "we have this treasure in earthen vessels." I suppose that fact (1) Modifies the treasure—owing to our sinful nature, our dull mind, our tired body, our fragile will, our fluctuating feelings, our frayed nerves, it becomes restricted in its operations. But I know that this fact (2) Magnifies the vessel—to think that God not only can, but will, take us up in His service in spite of our human weakness. In Psalm 39:4, David expresses his anxiety "that I may know how frail I am." Yes, better to know it and to guard against it. Yet (1) God chooses such. The Early Church was up against a stiff proposition—the wise, the mighty, the "things that are," or, as we should say, "the powers that be" and to counter and conquer them He quite deliberately "chose" very frail persons, as 1 Corinthians 1:27–28 states. Moreover (2) God uses such—Peter the boaster, Thomas the doubter, Philip the ignorant, John the fiery, you and me. He is prepared to use even such poor specimens as ourselves. Because (3) God infuses such— fills them with the Holy Spirit, that they may be, and do, what He purposes for them. The frail shall not fail—if filled. Having looked at the quite natural humanities, our passage unfolds to us—

Then—Divinities

Paul pens his last words to his son. So where shall he lead him, where leave him? Where shall he find for him a stable resting-place? First, in (*a*) *A Divine Presence*—"the Lord Jesus Christ be with your spirit." (1) Paul's own experience had, through a myriad perils, and adventures, and distresses, been very precious. Over and over again it had been his Master's presence which had saved him. Even in our last study, we saw him in perplexity because all who should have stood by him had forsaken him; but, in verse 17, we find him drawing his comfort and help from the blessed realization that the Lord stood with him. Paul might have driven home his lesson by recalling case after case of God's people throughout his prized Old Testament who had been similarly succored. For instance (2) Joseph's experience was so eminently remarkable. Genesis 39:2 had said that "the Lord was with Joseph, and he was a successful man"—or, in William Tyndale's vivid rendering, "he was a luckie fellowe." A lucky fellow? Listen: He is a slave, and in a foreign country, and knowing not a soul there, nor one word of the language! A lucky fellow, indeed! Yes, for the one all-sufficing reason that the Lord was with him. That was the overriding fact of his life, the overmastering secret of his success. And this shall be (3) Timothy's experience—he shall soon be bereft of his spiritual father's earthly presence; but he shall be stayed and established on that of his Heavenly Father. Looked at from the merely human and earthly standpoint, Timothy's situation was a by no means enviable one—his environment, with increasing persecution abroad, was gravely forbidding; his personality, somewhat timid and shrinking, and delicate in health, was scarcely "tough" enough to be expected to stand up to it all; his responsibilities, as the leader of the Christian forces in his area, the one to whom they would all naturally look for guidance, and inspiration, and example, would weigh down even the strongest. Yes, all true; but, Timothy, this also is true, that, in the hottest of the fire, you shall know the comfort of the Master's presence, even as three other young men did long years before you, when "the form of the fourth" meant so much (Daniel 3:25). And (4) Our experience shall, thank God, be the same. We, too, may count upon His presence, however difficult our circumstances may become.

That, then, is the first of the divinities to which Paul directs his young friend. The second is (*b*) *A Divine Power*—"grace be with you." Grace: what a word, and what a thing! Dr. Handley Moule defined it as "love in action." Our familiar hymn has accustomed us to the idea of "grace to cover all my sin"—that comes first, of course; but then we have "grace to cover all my need."

How tremendous, both in volume and in variety, was Timothy's need—and yours, too, perhaps. But how enormous is this vast supply. I am greatly interested in a Greek word which comes only twice in the New Testament, each time used by Peter and translated as "various" or "manifold." In 1 Peter 1:6 it is "various trials"—oh, how many are the trials and troubles and testings of life. How shall we stand firm? In 1 Peter 4:10, it is "manifold grace"—one grace in a myriad manifestations. Hold up your left hand and look upon the fingers and thumb as representative of the first "manifold" variety; and now your right, as picturing the second "manifold." As you view the one, bring across the other to cover it—exactly matching, you will observe, all the fingers and each of the fingers. And then take the illustration down into your very soul—that, on the one hand, the "manifold grace" is there to meet the "various trials" on the other hand, the shape and style of the grace exactly corresponding to the shape and style of the need. Note one last point: the "you" here is plural. It is usually translated "with you all": I venture diffidently to render it "with you and yours." The all-sufficient grace for pastor and people, for shepherd and flock alike. "Amen"!

So ends the letter of this father to this son. Tell me: have you any sons, any children in the faith, any that you have been enabled to bring to a saving knowledge of the Lord Jesus Christ as Paul brought Timothy and a thousand more? As you put down this book of studies, will you, if you have never begun before, start to long, and to labor, to be a soul winner—that you may have one, and many more than one, to bring up for Him and bring on in His ways. John Keble said, "The salvation of one soul is worth more than the framing of a Magna Charta of a thousand worlds." Indeed, as Proverbs 11:30 has it, "He who wins souls is wise"; and if you feel wholly inadequate for such a holy task, you must go and speak with Him about it—who said, in Matthew 4:19, "I will *make you* fishers of men." Of the famous Dr. Arnold, his eldest son, Matthew, wrote in his *Rugby Chapel*—

> *"But thou wouldst not alone*
> *Be saved, my father! alone*
> *Conquer and come to thy goal."*

Neither would Paul, who, in 1 Corinthians 9:22, wrote of his earnest longing "that I might by all means save some." Please, God, may our study together of this great letter lead us to the like frame of mind and to the like purpose of life.

This book was produced by CLC Publications. We hope it has been life-changing and has given you a fresh experience of God through the work of the Holy Spirit. CLC Publications is an outreach of CLC International, a global literature mission with work in over 50 countries. If you would like to know more about us or are interested in opportunities to serve with a faith mission, we invite you to contact us at:

CLC Ministries International
P.O. Box 1449
Fort Washington, PA 19034

Phone: (215) 542-1242
E-mail: clcmail@clcusa.org
www.clcusa.org

DO YOU LOVE GOOD CHRISTIAN BOOKS?
Do you have a heart for worldwide missions?

You can receive a FREE subscription to:
Floodtide,
(CLC's magazine on global literature missions).

Order by e-mail at:

floodtide@clcusa.org
or fill in the coupon below and mail to:

**P.O. Box 1449,
Fort Washington, PA 19034.**

```
┌─────────────────────────────────────────────┐
│        FREE FLOODTIDE SUBSCRIPTION!           │
│  Name: _____  │
│  Address: _____  │
│  _____  │
│  Phone: _____  E-mail: _____  │
└─────────────────────────────────────────────┘
```

READ THE REMARKABLE STORY OF
the founding of
CLC INTERNATIONAL

"Any who doubt that Elijah's God still lives ought to read of the money supplied when needed, the stores and houses provided and the appearance of personnel in answer to prayer.

—Moody Monthly

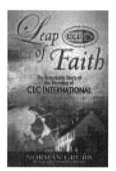

Is it possible that the printing press, the editor's desk, the Christian bookstore, and the mail order department, can glow with the fast-moving drama of an "Acts of the Apostles"?

Find out, as you are carried from two people in an upstairs bookroom to a worldwide chain of Christian bookcenters, multiplied by nothing but a "shoestring" of faith and committed, though unlikely, lives.

PHILIPPIANS - Joy Way — ISBN 0-87508-679-9

COLOSSIANS - True Life in Christ — ISBN 0-87508-683-7

1 TIMOTHY - A Leader Led — ISBN 0-87508-677-2

2 TIMOTHY - To My Son — ISBN 0-87508-685-3

JAMES - A Belief that Behaves — ISBN 0-87508-682-9

1 JOHN - The Fellowship — ISBN 0-87508-681-0